W9-DHM-523

Library of Shakespearean Biography and Criticism

I. PRIMARY REFERENCE WORKS ON SHAKESPEARE

II. CRITICISM AND INTERPRETATION

    A. Textual Treatises, Commentaries
    B. Treatment of Special Subjects
    C. Dramatic and Literary Art in Shakespeare

III. SHAKESPEARE AND HIS TIME

    A. General Treatises. Biography
    B. The Age of Shakespeare
    C. Authorship

Library of Shakespearean Biography and Criticism

Series III, Part B

SHAKESPEARE'S
STRATFORD

SHAKESPEARE'S
STRATFORD

By EDGAR I. FRIPP
A Life Trustee of Shakespeare's Birthplace

BOOKS FOR LIBRARIES PRESS
FREEPORT, NEW YORK

First Published 1928
Reprinted 1970

INTERNATIONAL STANDARD BOOK NUMBER:
0-8369-5506-4

LIBRARY OF CONGRESS CATALOG CARD NUMBER:
70-128886

PRINTED IN THE UNITED STATES OF AMERICA

PREFACE

A GREAT ARTIST, whether poet or painter, inevitably reflects his environment, while he mirrors so much more. Unconsciously and consciously he shows us the surroundings of his youth and manhood, the places, happenings, and people among whom he was born and bred, loved, worked, and suffered. We see medieval Florence in Dante's *Divina Commedia*: he would not have been Dante had he not revealed his beloved city. Stratford, and in a less degree London, lives in Shakespeare's work.

From first to last his native town was the Poet's home. Stratford was his refuge from an overcrowded life. Rehearsals and instruction (with distribution and final revision of the parts—not to mention the touching up of old or other men's work), acting in the afternoon and often in the evening, at Court and in the halls of nobles and scholars, at the Curtain, then at the Globe and the Blackfriars, left little leisure for dramatic composition. From the gathering of the players in London for the Christmas season to their flight into the country from summer heat and epidemic, and the conclusion of their tour, usually in the West, in or near Warwickshire, Shakespeare led an exhausting existence, and welcomed, we may believe, with an infinite relief, the quiet of Arden and Avon, the old fellowship of neighbours who were not 'players' but merely 'men and women', and the love which awaited him in Henley Street and New Place. The artist, even the great (the lesser almost invariably loses it at some time or another), is in danger of forfeiting his sanity, mistaking the imaginary for fact; and it is good to trace those simple, strong realities which enabled Shakespeare, amid thrilling and maddening experience, to maintain his magnificent common sense.

And Stratford was not unworthy of the Poet. I find it as interesting and alive, as rich in the clash of thought and character, as full of kind and wise if sometimes quaint humanity, as once, before I had studied it and merely accepted tradition and opinion, I supposed it mean and commonplace. To Mrs. C. C. Stopes we owe in large measure the challenge to the authority of the late Halliwell-Phillipps and his poor estimate (whatever his enthusiasm for documents) of the town and people. If I often do not agree with her,[1] I gratefully acknowledge the assistance I have derived from her fearless researches. Still more I am indebted to my old friend and fellow worker, the late Mr. Richard Savage. We went over the ground

[1] Curiously she identifies John Shakespeare corviser with the recusant, 'Master John Shakespeare', of 1592. She says, he 'had been made the master of the Shoemakers' Company. And it may be noted that in Stratford they always recognized the wives as well as the husbands as recusants. If our John' (the Poet's father) 'had been entered as a recusant, his wife would have been classed as one. The corviser's wife had died, and he himself shortly afterwards disappeared from the town, while our John lived on there till his fortunes turned. A later example may make this clear: Thomas Barker was removed from his office of Alderman because his wife is an obstinate recusant, and not to be re-elected unless his wife deny or alter her Religion' (*Shakespeare and the Theatre*, Shakespeare Association, 1927, p. 231). On the contrary, mastership of his craft would not entitle John the corviser to be called 'Master Shakespeare' by the churchwardens and commissioners for recusancy (Sir Thomas Lucy, Sir Fulke Greville, and the rest); wives as such were not presented at Stratford, or elsewhere, with their husbands (only four out of some two dozen are presented with their husbands), whereas certain wives (at least six) are presented without their husbands; John the corviser's wife (his third) was not dead in 1592, but very much alive, with three young children; and Mistress Barber was one of those presented for recusancy *without their husbands*. See p. 14 f.

together, geographical and documentary, and I think he would say of this little work, though it only touches the fringe of the subject, that it does some justice at last to Shakespeare's Stratford.

I disclaim, however, championship. Townsfolk had their faults as well as sterling virtues. Shakespeare must have suffered sometimes as did Master Anthony Langston, the Town Clerk elected in 1617 on the death of Francis Collins. He threw up his office once in despair, ' finding so much jealous heart-burning amongst the best of this borough, and being out of all hope of purification'. But he adds later, withdrawing his resignation with their approval, ' *revocatur ex consensu* '.[1] They were not so bad after all.

I am grateful to my fellow trustees of the Birthplace for permission to publish illustrations 4, 6, 7, 12, 13, 29, to the Stratford Corporation for illustrations 10 and 11, to Trust Houses Limited for illustration 2 (from a photograph by Mr. Herbert Felton), and to Mr. Paul Fripp, A.R.C.A., Director of Art at the Ladies' College, Cheltenham, for the illustrations (from his photographs) 1, 3, 8, 9, 14–28, 31–5, for his design of the Shakespeare Coat-of-Arms on the wrapper, and for his assistance in determining the character and relationship of the Droeshout portrait and engraving. Also I thank my friend, Mr. F. C. Wellstood, M.A., F.S.A., F.R.Hist.S., Secretary and Librarian of the Birthplace, for his valuable criticism.

STOW-ON-THE-WOLD.   E. I. F.

[1] Sept. 1620 (Council Book B, p. 392).

CONTENTS

LIST OF ILLUSTRATIONS

NOTE ON THE
STRATFORD-UPON-AVON CORPORATION

By the Charter of 1553 Stratford acquired a governing body of fourteen *Aldermen* and fourteen *Burgesses*. Aldermen alone elected aldermen, the whole body elected burgesses. Every year at Michaelmas the whole body elected from the aldermen a *Bailiff* and a *Sub-Bailiff* or *Head Alderman*, who were the leading borough magistrates during their term of office. They elected, also, from the burgesses two *Chamberlains*, who for two years in turn (though jointly responsible) had charge of the borough finances. They elected, also, from the general number of the townsmen, likely to approve themselves as suitable for burgess-ship, two *Tasters* or overseers of bread, meat, and beer sold in the borough, and four *Constables* for the maintenance of order and oversight of the watch. More permanent officials, though elected annually, were the two *Leather Sealers*, for the approval and stamping of leather offered for sale, and two *Serjeants-at-the-Mace*, in attendance, one on the Bailiff, the other on the Sub-Bailiff or Head Alderman, for the execution of their warrants and other orders. Serjeants wore their buff-leather uniform, and carried each his silver mace before him as the sign of his authority. Burgesses, Aldermen, Bailiff, and Deputy-Bailiff had their respective gowns of increasing cost. Distinction and rank were regarded on all sides. Aldermen were entitled to be called and addressed 'Master'. There was much decorum in the Town, with occasional fierce outbreak of temper, due chiefly to the religious conflict of the time.

1. THE BRIDGE

RIDING home from London or, after a tour in the west, from Gloucester, Shakespeare would enter Stratford by the already famous bridge built by Sir Hugh Clopton in the closing years of the fifteenth century. John Leland, who rode over it from Charlecote some twenty years before Shakespeare's birth, praised it as a 'great and sumptuous bridge' of stone, with 'fourteen arches and a long causey at the west end'. 'Afore the time of Hugh Clopton', he says, 'there was but a poor bridge of timber and no causey to it, whereby many poor folks and other refused to come to Stratford when Avon was up, or coming thither stood in jeopardy of life.'[1] Even stone could not always resist the flood when 'Avon was up'. In July 1588, the Armada summer, when the wet wind kept the Spanish fleet at the Groin and the English ships in harbour at Plymouth running short of provisions, the bridge was broken at both ends by flood. 'Three men going over' it, when they reached 'the middle could not go forwards', and returning 'could not go back, the water was so risen—it rose a yard every hour from eight to four'.[2] Willows, elms, and ashes were thick in the meadows at the country end, and they were hardly less thick in the town beyond.[3] Stratford, like Birmingham at this time, was embowered in trees.[4] On the town side of the bridge were the Bankcroft, a common for cattle and sheep, and pigs if they were ringed, and the Butt Close where patriotic burghers practised archery. In unobstructed view [5]

[1] *Itinerary*, Toulmin Smith, ii. 48 f.
[2] Memorandum in Welford Register.
[3] See the Survey of the Corporation Property made in 1582 (*Minutes and Accounts of Stratford-upon-Avon*, Dugdale Society, iii. 105–9).
[4] See the engraving of Birmingham in Dugdale's *Warwickshire*, 1656, p. 655.
[5] Without the islands (which have silted up since), the Tramway Bridge (built in 1826), and the Memorial Theatre (erected in 1879–83).

the river stretched away past barns and gardens to the stately Church, with its then short wooden spire.

Below the Church was the Mill, with its weir and fishing-ground. Tenant of the Mill until his death in 1583 was Alderman John Sadler; and lessee of the fishing-ground was Edward Ingram, then Robert Ingram his son, who had his boats, six 'putcheons' or eel-bucks, and his nets, a draught net and another called a 'trammel'.[1] Shakespeare was an angler, and knew both the Mill and the water beneath it full of perch and pike. He apparently did not use a fly, but he was familiar with bottom-fishing. He speaks of the worm for bait,[2] of the dace for pike,[3] and of giving line after striking.[4] That he sometimes used a net, we infer from a famous passage in *Macbeth*, I. vii. 1–7.

> If it were done when 'tis done, then 'twere well
> It were done *quickly*; if the assassination
> Could *trammel* up the consequence, and *catch*
> With his surcease success; that but this *blow*
> Might be the be-all and the end-all here,
> But here, *upon this bank and shoal* of Time,
> We'ld jump the life to come.

'Surcease' is legal, the inevitable, unconscious intrusion of the attorney's clerk;[5] the rest of the imagery is that of a fisherman expeditiously handling his rod and 'trammel' on the shallow sloping edge of a deep pool.

From Clopton Bridge a traveller would realize that Stratford was very much 'upon Avon' (*super Avonam*), and that the building of the 'stone bridge' was the making of Bridge Street. Passing through the Bargates (where he paid no toll)[6] he would face this main street, reaching up hill and dividing left and right into Fore Bridge Street and Back Bridge Street.

---

[1] Miscellaneous Documents, i. 52.   [2] *Hamlet*, IV. iii. 28–30.
[3] 2 *Henry IV*, III. ii. 356–8.   [4] *Winter's Tale*, I. ii. 180 f.
[5] p. 14 and note 2.   [6] Toll was not taken until 1701.

THE CLOPTON BRIDGE

(*The island and toll-gate are subsequent to Shakespeare*)

SCENE FROM WALL-PAINTING IN HOUSE IN ROTHER MARKET

Tobit and his wife, Anna, take leave of their son, Tobias, and his companion, Raphael (disguised), on their departure for Rages. The costume is of the time of Shakespeare's birth. Notice the hats, close-cut hair, moustaches and short beards, ruffs and wristlets ; Tobit's gown (of black velvet edged with gold) with high collar, and his gloves, Anna's coif and gown (of black velvet) over a dress of (gold) brocade : the (yellow) doublet with (red) sleeves and (orange) pantaloons of Tobias, Raphael's cloak and (purple) breeches, and their hose and low-heeled pointed shoes

2. 'THE SWAN' AND 'THE BEAR'

AT the bottom of the main street at opposite corners, right and left, stood the two chief inns of the town, the *Swan* and the *Bear*. The *Swan* was kept in succession by Thomas Dixon *alias* Waterman, father and son. The father was a glover as well as innkeeper, and an alderman. His wife was from Snitterfield, the birthplace of John Shakespeare, the Poet's father; and it is not unlikely that John Shakespeare served his apprenticeship with him as a glover, and owed to him, as a leading townsman, something of his early prosperity and speedy promotion to the Town Council. The son was also an alderman, but he fell out with the Council and left it in 1590. He married three times, and his third wife was Mistress Joan Sadler, widow of Alderman John Sadler of the Mill below the Church.

Harrison's praise of the Elizabethan Inn in Holinshed,[1] about the year 1587, is more than confirmed by what we know of the *Swan* from a valuable inventory made in 1603.[2] It was such a house as Sir Thomas Lucy or Sir Fulke Greville (both of them stayed there frequently), or even the lame and corpulent Earl of Warwick (on occasion),[3] might, like Falstaff, 'take his ease' in.[4] Windows were glazed with leaded panes, walls were wainscoted or hung with 'painted-cloths'. The subjects of these cloths were probably scriptural, such as Shakespeare speaks of, and like that of the mural paintings fresh and new in William Perrott's tavern in Rother Market [5]—the story, in Tudor costume, of Tobias and the Angel. The furniture was hand-made and, however primitive, a work of art. Oak cup-

[1] *Chronicles*, ii (1587), ' Description of England '.
[2] Miscellaneous Documents, vii. 31. Halliwell-Phillipps was mistaken in thinking it an inventory of effects at the *Bear* (*Outlines*, i. 139, 142).
[3] 'Paid for charges at the *Swan* the fifth of October when my Lord of Warwick was here' (Chamberlains' Account, presented 11 Jan.158¾).
[4] 1 *Henry IV*, III. iii. 92 f.   [5] Now embodied in the *White Swan*.

boards and tables, stools, a desk, chests, coffers, four-post bedsteads, with trundle or truckle-beds[1] beneath, were in keeping with the open beams of the ceiling and the naked floor. We notice 'waled' and other mattresses, flaxen and hempen sheets, blankets, feather-beds, coverlets of Arras, Dornix (of Tourney), and Turkey; 'twilly' and tapestry, 'dowle', 'red-thrummed'[2] and 'woven stuff'—one 'coverlet of Arras in the fair chest in the maids' chamber' was valued at £3. The chief rooms (as at the Boar's Head in East Cheap)[3] had their names and signs—the Lion, Talbot, and 'Dixon's', which like the Chamber of Shakespeare's Lucrece,[4] were combined bed-and-sitting rooms, and the Cock which was a sitting-room only. They were rich in cushions, of Turkey-work, woollen-list, tapestry, velvet, and satin. Napery was abundant, including napkins, much in request in the absence of forks. Silver consisted of a goblet gilt and five bowls, five spoons, and a salt gilt. Spoons otherwise were of latten, as were candlesticks and basins. Most utensils were of pewter Platters were of wood. Brass made a brave show—pots and pans, 'posnets', 'skillets' (legged saucepans), and other things. The kitchen must have been a delight. We observe on the premises 'three linen-wheels and a reel', and 'a great spinning wheel', and many articles familiar to students of Shakespeare—such as leather bottles, lanthorns, an old leather jack, a powdering-tub, and a boulting-hutch (which Falstaff resembled),[5] a whetstone, pairs of bellows, a close-stool, a christening-sheet (or child's bearing-cloth) and 'a face-cloth' (a costly piece of embroidery laid on the face of the dead);

[1] Mercutio professed to sleep in a truckle-bed (*Romeo and Juliet*, II. i. 39).
[2] Made of the 'thrums' or loose-ends of the weaver's warp. Mistress Ford's maid's fat aunt of Brentford wore a hat of this coarse material which Falstaff gladly commandeered (*Merry Wives*, IV. ii. 77–80).
[3] 1 *Henry IV*, II. iv. 30 ('Half Moon'), 42 ('Pomgarnet').
[4] With its writing table (l. 1,290) and painting (ll. 1,367 ff.).
[5] 1 *Henry IV*, II. iv. 495.

wicker bottles, a tun-dish, and a warming-pan; besoms, a fosset (not for drawing liquor but for holding money), querns for malt and mustard, billets of wood, and a leaden 'tod-stone' (for weighing). There are articles, also, which the Poet does not mention—a trivet, a well-drag (for getting things up which have fallen into the well, living things sometimes), and a soap-barrel.

Awful thought! Shakespeare never mentions *soap*. What a picture presents itself to the 'biographical' mind! Did the 'Stratford boor' never wash? Was he content, like King James, to wipe his fingers' ends with a wet napkin? [1] Let us be calm. There were points of resemblance between the King's player and His Majesty. Both loved a horse (though Shakespeare when he rode had not to be tied on),[2] both had a taste (of a sort) for the drama, and a distaste for tobacco[3] (Shakespeare does not name it). But there all likeness vanishes. The Poet was as healthy in his habits, without doubt, as King James was unwholesome. He had faith in 'the health-giving air'[4] and 'the blessed sun',[5] in the free movement of the heart and lungs,[6] in exercise,[7] in change of scene,[8] rest and sleep,[9] in 'keeping the teeth clean',[10] in 'honest water',[11] to drink

[1] Weldon, *The Court and Character of King James*, p. 165.
[2] 'He was trussed on horse back, and as he was set so would he ride'; Coke, *Detection*, p. 71.
[3] See the royal *Counterblast to Tobacco*, 1604.
[4] *2 Henry IV*, IV. iv. 116; *Measure for Measure*, II. iv. 24–6; *Love's Labour's Lost*, I. i. 236.
[5] *Taming of the Shrew*, IV. v. 17 f.; *1 Henry IV*, I. ii. 10; II. iv. 449.
[6] *Richard III*, IV. i. 34 f.; *Antony and Cleopatra*, I. iii. 71; *Winter's Tale*, III. ii. 174 f.
[7] *Love's Labour's Lost*, I. i. 233–7; *Cymbeline*, I. i. 110; *Winter's Tale*, IV. iv. 790.
[8] *Romeo and Juliet*, I. i. 231–4; I. ii. 46–57, 90–2, 99–104; *King Lear*, II. iv. 106–13 (a remarkable passage, as pointed out by Sir St. Clair Thomson in a lecture at Stratford on 23 April 1923).
[9] *Macbeth*, I. ii. 35–43; *King Lear*, III. vi. 104 f.; IV. vii. 12–18, &c., &c.
[10] *Coriolanus*, II. iii. 67.
[11] *Timon of Athens*, I. ii. 59 f.; Shakespeare's one good word for wine (as a means of cheerfulness) is in *Henry VIII*, I. iv. 5–7.

and to bathe in. He sends the boy to school with 'shining morning face',[1] has not a little to say about washing the face and hands,[2] and of the folly of face-painting;[3] one of his greatest scenes is of a lady trying to remove a stain from her fingers.[4] He was unquestionably a swimmer—had swum in the Avon as a boy 'on bladders beyond his depth',[5] had 'plunged' as a youth with 'lusty sinews', in response to a challenge, into 'the angry flood' (and the Avon could be as angry as Tiber), and 'buffeted it, throwing it aside, and stemming it with heart of controversy'.[6] Such language is not that of an onlooker, however envious, but of enthusiastic participation.

There was no bathroom at the *Swan*, but we observe 'ewers and basins' and 'forty-nine hempen towels'; and Mistress Dixon *alias* Waterman had a tub of hot water before a good fire for the weary and bespattered rider at the end of his thirty miles.

Soap, like bread,[7] beer, and tallow, was a home-product, one of the accomplishments of a good housekeeper. So numerous were these handicrafts (including spinning and making bone-lace) that we are not surprised if she had little time (like Shakespeare's daughter, Mistress Hall)[8] for reading and writing.

Two series of items in the inventory remain—the contents of the cellar, and of Alderman Dixon's wardrobe.

The cellar held 'three tierces of claret-wine' valued at £13, 'two butts of sack' at £34, 'six hogsheads of beer' at £3, and 'certain remnants of red-wine, white-wine, and vinegar at £1. The prominence of sack, the generic name for Spanish and Canary vintages, is remarkable. Once only does Shakespeare speak of claret-wine; upwards of fifty times he refers to sack—frequently on the lips of its great apologist and victim, Falstaff.

---

[1] *As You Like It*, II. vii. 146.   [2] *Coriolanus*, II. iii. 66, &c.
[3] *Love's Labour's Lost*, IV. iii. 258–73; *Timon of Athens*, IV. iii. 147, &c.
[4] *Macbeth*, V. I.
[5] *Henry VIII*, III. iii. 358–61.   [6] *Julius Caesar*, I. ii. 100–11.
[7] Such bread, as gives us an appetite to think of.
[8] See Doctor Cooke's preface to the *Select Observations*, 1657.

Sack was the fashionable beverage of the gentry, as home-brewed ale was the common drink of the people. It was taken as a *liqueur*, chiefly in hot or cold water sweetened with sugar. Spirits—such as *aqua vitae*, to which Juliet's old nurse was addicted,[1] and *usquebaugh*, which Shakespeare does not mention—apparently were not sold at the *Swan*. They were procurable at the tavern—Burbage's in Bridge Street, Atwood's (afterwards Thomas Quyney's) in High Street, William Perrott's in Rother Market, or the 'Shrieve's House' in Sheep Street.[2]

Alderman Dixon was not regardless of his personal appearance. He had two gowns and 'everything handsome about him'. The gowns, of his burgess-ship and his aldermanship,[3] may have been heirlooms from his father. One was of sheep's wool furred with fox (valued at 30*s*.), the other a costly robe (valued at £5) 'of brown, blue-lined with lamb and faced with foins'. He possessed a suit of fustian (doublet and breeches, valued, with a pair of stockings, at 15*s*.), perhaps made of the 'Milan fustian' which he obtained at the shop of Francis Smith junior shortly before his death; a coat of medley cloth (16*s*.), a green jerkin (20*s*.), a cloak of tuft taffeta (30*s*.), and a French tawny cloak (20*s*.). Besides these, and a jerkin of Spanish leather, he possessed ten shirts, thirteen ruff-bands for his neck and wrists, a girdle with a purse, a sword and buckler and 'skein', a pistol, a hat, a cap, a pair of shoes, two pairs of boots, and last but not least in those days of draughts and curtains, a night-cap.

Of the *Bear Inn*, which probably took its sign from the 'Bear and Ragged Staff' of the Dudleys, I must say a few words

[1] *Romeo and Juliet*, III. ii. 88; IV. 5. 16.
[2] There was a deplorable increase in the consumption of spirits between the reigns of Elizabeth and Anne. Defoe is always giving Robinson Crusoe 'a dram'.
[3] Later (in 1654) the official attire of Aldermen and Burgesses was distinguished as 'gown' and 'cloak' (Council Book C, p. 405).

because of its interesting host, Thomas Barber. For more than half a century Barber was identified with the *Bear* (he was known as 'Barber of the Bear') and with the Stratford Corporation. He was universally respected, notwithstanding that he was from time to time 'suspect' on account of the recusancy of his first wife, and then of his second, who were both Roman Catholics. Three times he was bailiff of Stratford, and he would probably have served for a fourth period if the pronounced religious opinions of his second wife had not rendered his tenure of the office impossible. Stratford at this time was an ultra-Protestant borough, under the influence of its late bishops, Latimer and Hooper (both of whom were martyrs), of Sir Thomas Lucy, the Earl of Warwick, and Thomas Cartwright (master of Leicester Hospital in Warwick), and a succession of vicars and schoolmasters appointed by the Earl of Warwick.

Whatever doubts were entertained of Barber's loyalty he proved a doughty champion of Town rights, first against the lord of the manor, Sir Edward Greville, then against the Combes. He won the grateful recognition of the puritan Town Clerk, Shakespeare's cousin, Thomas Greene, who notes in his diary his opinion and example, quotes his conversation, and at length writes the entry, with a big mark against it as an event of significance to the borough and himself:

'1615 14 Augusti. Master Barber died'.

The old man had buried his Catholic wife, Joan, four days previously. Together they were interred within the church (it was his right as an alderman) in some spot now unknown. We read in the register the successive entries:

'Aug. 10 Joane vxor Thomas Barber gentlewoman.
Aug. 15 Thomas Barber gentleman.'

We have reason to think of him as a 'gentleman'.

All his life, then, until a few months before his death, Shakespeare knew Master Barber. After the old man's decease he sent a messenger, one James (who was probably Greene's clerk, Peter James *alias* Taylor), on Thursday 5 September 1615, to his executors to discuss and 'agree with them' as to the course they should take to protect 'Master Barber's interest' against the Combes.[1]

3. THE PLAYERS IN STRATFORD

A NOTEWORTHY feature of Inn life, in Stratford as in Warwick, Coventry, Gloucester, and other towns, demands attention before we leave the *Swan* and the *Bear*. Companies of players from time to time rode into the borough, with blowing of trumpets, and making their way to the house of the Bailiff, waited upon him to inform him what nobleman's or knight's livery they wore, and request his permission to perform in public. If the Bailiff approved, and would show respect for their master, he appointed them to give an exhibition of their quality before himself and his brethren of the Corporation in the Gild Hall. This was called the Bailiff's play, where every one that would and could 'might go in without money', a collection being afterwards taken from the audience, which the Bailiff would supplement as he thought fit from the Chamberlain's purse. Public performances followed at the inn where the players lodged, a stage being erected in the yard and a charge made for admission.

Of Master Dixon's attitude towards such visitors we have no knowledge, but Master Barber was more than friendly. In his

[1] The *Bear* passed from the Sadlers to Anthony Nash, who bequeathed it in 1622 to his son, Thomas Nash, the future husband (in 1626) of Shakespeare's granddaughter, Elizabeth Hall. It was burned or taken down before 10 Oct. 1647, when a fine was levied on its site, 'where the *Bear* in Bridge St. formerly stood'. The *Swan* disappeared in 1754, when two large houses were erected on its site facing the Bridge.

first bailiwick he welcomed two companies, in his second, which was the memorable year of Shakespeare's probable joining the players, 1586–7, no less than four and perhaps five.

Shakespeare's father when Bailiff in 1568–9 gave permission to two companies, the Queen's Men, whom he rewarded liberally, and the Earl of Worcester's Men, whom he damned with faint praise, giving them a shilling, the lowest reward on record in the annals of the borough. He was a man always of decided opinions.[1] Between that date and the year of Barber's second bailiwick, twenty-two visits were paid to the town by players, and Shakespeare as a boy and a man had ample opportunity of witnessing some of the best acting in England. The Earl of Worcester's company, of which Edward Alleyn was already a leading member, came to Stratford in 1583–4, and it is not unlikely that Alleyn's acquaintance with Shakespeare began then.[2] In 1587, during Barber's bailiwick, the two most distinguished companies of the time visited the town and probably performed at the *Bear*. These were the Queen's Men, which included the famous actor Richard Tarleton, and his more refined colleague in comedy, Thomas Wilson; and the Earl of Leicester's Men, of whom William Kemp was the leading spirit. Leicester's company at the moment was short-handed, owing to the absence of members in Germany, and I will venture the belief that at Kemp's invitation Shakespeare, aged three-and-twenty, 'being', as Aubrey says, 'inclined to poetry and acting' (and, as he might have added, to music), left his lawyer's office and joined the players. Aubrey is the earliest and best biographer (if he can be called such), and he says that Shakespeare 'did act exceedingly well'. He knows nothing of a runaway poacher story.

[1] *Minutes and Accounts*, II.xliv–xlviii, III.xl–xlii. He was contentious—even in his welcome remark about his son: 'Will is a good honest fellow, but I durst crack a jest with him at any time' (Plume MSS.).
[2] He was probably at Leicester with Worcester's Men on 6 March 1584.

4. THE RUNAWAY POACHER LEGEND

THAT legend on examination 'melts into thin air'—*in tenuem evanescit auram.*[1] Shakespeare's knowledge of the chase, and his delight in it, were acquired at Clopton, or any one or more of the half-dozen deer-parks in the neighbourhood; certainly *not* at Charlecote, where there was no park until the latter half of the seventeenth century. Sir Thomas Lucy's venison, it appears, was brought by a keeper over a horse's back from his wife's park forty miles away at Sutton near Tenbury in Worcestershire. There is no record of the gift of a buck by a Lucy to the Stratford Corporation in the lifetime of Shakespeare. The donors of this annual present were usually the Grevilles. Nor is there any trace of a suit by Sir Thomas against the youthful poet. The latter, moreover, would have been singularly wanting in the discretion with which he is universally credited, to have gone out of his way to make an enemy of the most honoured and influential magnate of the district. The story, we need not doubt, originated in the opening scene of the *Merry Wives of Windsor*, with which it is connected by the earliest anecdotist responsible for the tale nearly a century after the supposed event.[2]

No *contemporary*, in the least acquainted with Lucy, could have identified him with Shallow of *Henry IV*. Between that chattering old dotard, four-score and upward, unable to speak two consecutive sentences of English, eking out his feeble utterance with musty Romanist expletives ('by the rood', 'by the mass', 'God's liggens', 'Cock and pie', and the rest), bragging on the edge of the grave of the licentious follies of his youth at Clement's Inn, 'every third word a lie', close-fisted, mean, disreputable; and the cultivated builder and master of Charlecote House, the private pupil of John Foxe, friend as I find, of

[1] To quote a line of the *Aeneid* (iv. 278, ix. 658) translated by Shakespeare (*Tempest*, IV. i. 150).
[2] The parson Davies of Sapperton sometime before 1708.

Thomas Ashton (the famous head of Shrewsbury School);[1] probably the ablest public man, not excepting Sir Fulke Greville, in Warwickshire, greatly trusted by the Privy Council, appointed by them on innumerable commissions, writer in a fine hand of reports and dispatches, recipient more than once of the Queen's special thanks for his efficient services, honoured and loved in Stratford, called in to help in any difficult and delicate negotiation, devoted, moreover, to the wife of his youth—Mistress Joyce Acton, whose father, Thomas Acton, friend and 'gossip' of Latimer, was great-great-grandson of Sir Roger Acton, hanged in 1414 for complicity in the so-called plot of the Lollard, Sir John Oldcastle: between that Shallow and this Lucy, I venture to say, there is not a ghost of resemblance. But the Shallow of the *Merry Wives*, like the Falstaff and Quickly, stands somewhat apart from his former self, a fussy irascible appendage to his kinsman Slender, the unsuccessful woer of Mistress Anne Page; and if, as is practically certain, the *Merry Wives* was written for the pleasure of the old Queen at Windsor in 1601, a twelvemonth after Lucy's death, there may possibly be a gibe in the punning on *luce* and *louse*, *coat* and *cod*, at the new and unpopular master of Charlecote, Sir Thomas Lucy the second, who gave mortal offence this summer at Stratford. High Sheriff of Warwickshire, he supported the extortionate lord of the manor, Sir Edward Greville, in his crazy action for 'riot' against the Corporation for their defence of Bankcroft. Shakespeare's friends Quyney, Walker, and Sadler among others were arrested and conveyed to the Marshalsea, and his cousin Thomas Greene was their legal adviser.[2] All this was enough to make old Lucy turn in his grave.[3]

[1] He stayed with Lucy at Charlecote in 1571 (*S. P. Dom. Eliz.* lxxxi. 52). Philip Sidney and Fulke Greville were among his pupils.
[2] *Master Richard Quyney*, pp. 170 f., 177–80.
[3] The 'Sir Thomas Lucy' whose portrait appears in the Cambridge New Shakespeare *Merry Wives*, 'from a miniature at Charlecote', with

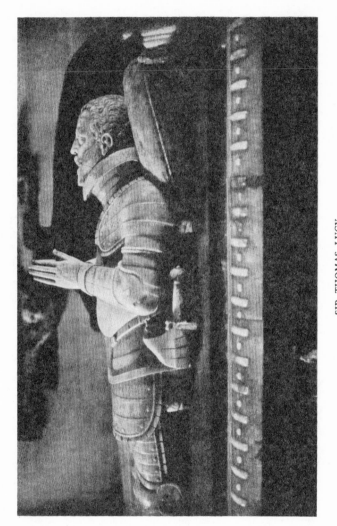

SIR THOMAS LUCY
(from his effigy in Charlecote Church)

THE HIGH CROSS FROM WOOD STREET IN 1820

(from a lithograph by C. F. Green)

On the extreme right is the gatehouse of the Hill-Sturley premises. On the extreme left are the house with Dutch gable and the half-timber house facing the west end of Middle Row. On opposite corners of Fore Bridge Street are houses on the sites of the 'Corner House' (Smith) and the 'Cage' (Quyney). The large house (with eight windows) on the right-hand side of Fore Bridge Street is on the site of the Crown Inn

5. BRIDGE STREET

BUT to return to Stratford. Fore Bridge Street and Back Bridge Street were parted by Middle Row. In Fore Bridge Street on the left was the third inn of the town, a borough property called the *Crown*[1] (which name was significantly changed during the Commonwealth to *Woolsack*).[2] Above the *Crown*, at the corner of Fore Bridge Street and High Street, was a house called the *Cage*, on the site of an ancient prison. Opposite the *Cage* in Middle Row was Burbage's tavern. Half-way up Middle Row was the 'Chure', a passage connecting Back Bridge Street with Fore Bridge Street and, proceeding through the *Crown*, Fore Bridge Street with High Street, where it emerged at the gate-house of the Gaol[3]—an old Episcopal house of detention, now the borough lock-up, not to be confused with the *Cage*, though probably once connected with it.

At the 'Chure' in Middle Row were the 'Shambles', and the shop (or rather shops) of Alderman Rafe Cawdrey, a butcher and a Catholic, whose wife and daughters were recusants and his son a fugitive Jesuit priest. He was tenant under the Corporation of the fourth inn of the town, an ancient hostel, the property of the Gild, rebuilt by them in 1467–9, the *Angel*, at the top of Back Bridge Street on the right, adjoining Henley Street.[4] A little below the 'Chure', on the right, in Back Bridge Street,[5] was the house of Henry Field, tanner, father of Richard Field the printer in London. William Shakespeare

mild eyes, raised brows, broad lids, long slender nose, spade beard, long hair hiding his ears over broad collar, is Sir Thomas the Third— not Sir Thomas the First of Shakespeare's youth, who had a vigorous and even grim countenance, as we may see in the effigy on his tomb, with short beard, a close-cropped hair (a 'round-head'), short nose, thick nostrils, determined mouth, and plenty of forehead.

[1] On the site of nos. 12–14.
[2] Stratford supported the Parliament. See pp. 72 n., 76 f.
[3] Between nos. 4 and 5.   [4] See p. 15.
[5] On the site of no. 28.

and Richard Field were doubtless schoolfellows in Stratford, the latter being the senior by two and a half years.[1] Field was apprenticed to the well-known Huguenot printer in the Black-friars, Thomas Vautrollier, in 1579, about the time that Shakespeare, as I believe, began his articles in the office of the Town Clerk (Sir Thomas Lucy's agent at Sherborne), Master Henry Rogers.[2] Both youths were excellently grounded in Latin, and Field in Vautrollier's household learned French. Field married his master's widow, succeeded to the business (in 1588) and prospered; published Latin and French books as well as English, and among English books certain works of great interest to Shakespeare, possibly at his suggestion and recommendation—such as Puttenham's *Arte of English Poesie* in 1589, when it had been some four years in manuscript and rejected (after entry at Stationers' Hall in 1588) by at least one publisher. He printed and published Shakespeare's early poems, *Venus and Adonis* (in 1593) and *Lucrece* (in 1594). It is infinitely to be regretted that Heminge and Condell did not entrust to him (probably on account of pirated copyright) the production of the Folio of Shakespeare's Plays of 1623. He was then at the head of his profession, and few printers' work in English, Latin, or French, was more accurate. We should have had a much better text of Shakespeare.

Three doors above Henry Field in Back Bridge Street on the same side[3] lived John Shakespeare the corviser, who must not be confused with Master John Shakespeare the father of William. John the corviser, who came from Warwick and was almost certainly a young kinsman of the Alderman,[4] did not attain to the latter's social status, was never 'Master Shakespeare', or a member of the Stratford Corporation, though he

[1] He was baptized on 16 Nov. 1561.
[2] *Minutes and Accounts of the Corporation of Stratford-upon-Avon 1553–1620*, III. xlii–xlviii.
[3] On the site of no. 25.
[4] Both their families may have come from Balsall.

FROM THE MAP OF WARWICKSHIRE OF 1603

It will be observed that there is no park at Charlecote, nor at Fulbrooke by Barford

served as a 'taster' and a 'constable'. Alderman Shakespeare, not the corviser, appraised Henry Field's goods on his death in 1592. The corviser, who took for his second wife Widow Roberts of Stratford, and succeeded to her late husband's business in Back Bridge Street, in 1584, had children by a third wife in Stratford,[1] who were named Ursula (probably godchild of Henry Field's wife), Humfrey, and Philip. He returned to Warwick about 1594, and died there in 1624.

6. HENLEY STREET

PAST the *Angel* we come to the house, the first in Henley Street,[2] of a notable man, William Smith, haberdasher and yeoman. I believe he was Shakespeare's godfather.[3] He was industrious and prosperous, desperately obstinate (like the Poet's father), continually at war with somebody, and defiant, if need be, of the Corporation. He lived to see at least three of his sons on the way to 'gentlehood', though you might think at times that he had not a penny to bless himself with—a trait also shared by Alderman Shakespeare.[4]

Next door but one to William Smith lived Alderman George Whateley,[5] a woollen-draper and yeoman, and an ancient member of the Corporation. He had land in Henley-in-Arden (his native town where he endowed in 1586 an elementary School to teach thirty children reading, writing, and arithmetic), and two brothers, fugitive Catholic priests, who hovered about Henley, and to whom he paid secret annuities, 'Sir Robert' and 'Sir John'. Twice he was Bailiff, and for many years as warden he had charge of Clopton Bridge. A few doors from Whateley's was the house of Gilbert Bradley,[6] a glover, Alderman Shakespeare's fellow craftsman, who probably stood

---

[1] See Preface, p. vi n. [2] Now Lambert's.
[3] *Minutes and Accounts*, I. lii.
[4] *Ib.* xl. Court of Record proceedings 12, 26 Feb., 12 Mar., 23 Apr., 7 May, 4 and 18 June, 10 Sept. 1589, 8 Apr. 1590.
[5] On the site of 3 and 4. [6] On the site of the Public Library.

godfather, at the baptism of William Shakespeare's brother Gilbert in 1566. Before Bradley's house was the 'cross-gutter', or covered channel, wherein a stream from Welcombe (?) called the 'Mere' crossed Henley Street to Mere Lane, on its way to Rother Market, and thence to Chapel Lane, and by New Place to the Avon.[1] Below this stream in Henley Street stood Hornby's smithy,[2] then a pair of cottages owned by an eccentric tailor named Wedgewood,[3] then the block of three houses owned by Alderman Shakespeare. We probably have a sketch of Wedgewood in his slippers haranguing Hornby in *King John*:

> I saw a smith stand with his hammer, thus,
> The whilst his iron did on the anvil cool,
> With open mouth swallowing a tailor's news;
> Who, with his shears and measure in his hand,
> Standing on slippers,—which his nimble haste
> Had falsely thrust upon contrary feet (IV. ii. 193–8).

Leaving Alderman Shakespeare's for a moment we will notice the house beyond of George Badger the woollen-draper,[4] an interesting and well-connected townsman, obstinate on the Catholic side, as, I do not doubt, Alderman Shakespeare, William Smith, and Alderman Wheeler of Henley Lane, were obstinate Protestants. Beyond Badger's was the house of a yeoman, John Ichiver, which was rebuilt after the great fire of 1594 as an inn by one Robert Johnson. On the other side of the street,[5] opposite Alderman Shakespeare, lived shepherds— John Cox and John Davies. Shepherds were dear to Shakespeare, and we will note them when we meet with them—

---

[1] Such was the opinion of the late Richard Savage. Halliwell-Phillipps says the mere ran from Rother Street across Henley Street into the Gild Pits and thence into the Avon near the Bridge (*Outlines*, ii. 157). The present surface-level somewhat supports Savage's view, as does the probable connexion of the stream in Dead Lane with that in Rother Street.   [2] On the site of the Birthplace ticket-office.
[3] *Minutes and Accounts*, II. xliii f.
[4] See p. 37 f. and *Master Richard Quyny*, pp. 107, 113–16, 122.
[5] On the site of nos. 46–9.

Hugh Smith (Alderman Cawdrey's shepherd) in Rother Market, Walter Hill in Church Street, Robert Stevens in Sheep Street, Richard Cowper in Wood Street, Thomas Alee in Wood Street (Alderman Wheeler's shepherd), and last but not least, Thomas Whittington in Shottery. Cox and Whittington were friends of the Hathaways.[1] Whittington lived at Hewland Farm with Mistress Shakespeare's father, Richard Hathaway *alias* Gardner, until the latter's death in 1581,[2] and then with her stepmother, Joan Hathaway *alias* Gardner, until her death in 1599. He died in 1601, leaving forty shillings of his savings in the hand of Mistress Shakespeare in trust for the poor.[3] Did the Poet find in this faithful old retainer of his wife's family (who had saved £50 at the time of his death) the prototype of his Adam or Corin in *As You Like It* ?

Orlando addresses Adam—

> O good old man, how well in thee appears
> The constant service of the antique world,
> When service sweat for duty, not for meed!
> Thou art not for the fashion of these times,
> Where none will sweat but for promotion.[4]

And Corin, on the defensive against Touchstone's humorous sophistry, replies:

> Sir, I am a true labourer: I earn that I eat, get that I wear, owe no man hate, envy no man's happiness, glad of other men's good, content with my harm; and the greatest of my pride is to see my ewes graze and my lambs suck.'[5]

There was not a little of this sound wisdom in Stratford.

[1] Cox, who left £73, made bequests to the widow and children of Thomas Hathaway in 1600.
[2] See Richard Hathaway's Will in *Minutes and Accounts*, iii. 86–90.
[3] A bequest strangely misinterpreted by Lee (*Life*, p. 280).
[4] II. iii. 56–60 (and see the old man's declaration, 38–55). Adam is as dear to Shakespeare as Jaques is offensive.
[5] III. ii. 77–81.

Near Cox in Henley Street dwelt a 'mettle-man' or tinker, a Welshman (and I suspect a puritan), Thomas a Pryce, whose son (or other kinsman), Michael a Pryce, Alderman Shakespeare befriended most generously in 1586, riding to Coventry (though he had to return the same or next day, 20 July, to serve on a jury)[1] in order to be surety for him in the large sum of £10 to answer to a charge of felony. This sum he afterwards lost by the faithless Michael's non-appearance.[2] Alderman Shakespeare had money to lose in matters which touched him charitably or religiously (and that in those days meant politically),[3] when he would resist to the utmost the payment of a debt or fine wherein he felt a grievance.[4]

There were tenements also that side of Henley Street in the occupation of Alderman Wheeler, Alderman Shakespeare's well-to-do fellow rebel in the Corporation, and colleague in recusancy, I do not doubt puritan recusancy, in 1592. They were both presented for not going to church as afraid of arrest for debt.[5] In Wheeler's case at least it seems ridiculous.[6] In Henley Street moreover lived Rafe Shaw and Peter Smart. Shaw was a 'wool-driver' (a buyer and seller of wool, *driving* it to market) and doubtless had his 'wool-house' (as Master Reynolds had his in Corn Street).[7] John Shakespeare appraised his goods on his death in 1592[8] (notwithstanding the plea that he was afraid to show himself at church). Shaw's widow married the Schoolmaster, Aspinall;[9] and his son

---

[1] Court of Record Register.
[2] Queen's Bench, Controlment Roll, 223, m. 44.
[3] Religion and politics were inseparably associated.   [4] See p. 30.
[5] The Serjeant could arrest a defendant in church if he could not find him on a week-day. John Shakespeare does not seem to have been undiscoverable. See p. 14 f.
[6] He was a man of very considerable property. See *Minutes and Accounts*, III. lvii–lx.
[7] See p. 41. I cannot find the term 'wool-shop' in the records, or that John Shakespeare had either a 'woolshop' or a woolhouse (*Outlines*, i. 377).   [8] Misc. Doc. vii. 142.   [9] p. 50.

Julines (Julins, Julyne, July; not Julius, which was a different name), became William Shakespeare's next-door neighbour but one at New Place and witness to his will in 1616. Peter Smart was brother of the foretime schoolmaster and vicar of Stratford, William Smart, a graduate of Cambridge and Fellow of Christ's. Peter proved himself something of a scholar as the Borough Chamberlain. He had a son, William, who became a tailor. No craft stood higher in the reign of Elizabeth than the tailor's. William Smart made the livery of the lord-of-the-manor's men, Sir Edward Greville's: which livery consisted of a hare-coloured cloak, with velvet and silver lace.[1] In Stratford, as elsewhere, men and women spent on clothes, plain or gay, and part of their attire, on Sundays and week-days, was gloves.

7. THE BIRTHPLACE

GLOVE-MAKING was an old and leading industry in the town, and the seven glovers in John Shakespeare's 'brotherhood' had the place of honour, for the sale of their wares, at the Market-Cross. John had so prospered at his craft[2] that he purchased a house and shop in Henley Street before his marriage with Mary Arden (probably we should say 'Mistress Arden') in 1557. This tenement was the East House of the three which he ultimately owned.[3] The Middle and West Houses he bought in 1575, and there is no evidence but the tradition of the 'Birthroom' that he occupied either prior to that date. The Poet was born, I believe, with his brothers Gilbert and Richard, and his sisters Joan and Anne, in the East House, and only Edmund, the youngest child, first saw the light in the Middle House. The tradition of the 'Birthroom' in the Middle House may be explained by the fact that after his father's death

[1] Misc. Doc. vi. 74, 99, 102.
[2] I think he may have succeeded to the business of Alderman Dixon, which was not pursued by the latter's family.
[3] *Minutes and Accounts*, i. 57.

in 1601 the Poet let, and practically gave, the Middle House (and what was left of the West House) to his sister, Joan Hart, and her descendants, *and leased the East House to strangers.* In course of time the house of the Harts was regarded as the ancestral home.[1]

In the great fire of 1594, which destroyed nearly the whole of Henley Street, the Shakespeare-block was saved, so far as it was saved, by the presence of the stream (or 'mere') above Hornby's smithy, and by vigorous use, probably, of fire-hooks[2] on the West House, which detached it, or what remained of it, and the adjoining Middle and East Houses, from the burning premises below. Bradley's house and the dwellings of Badger and Ichiver (or Johnson) were burned down. John Shakespeare did not rebuild the West House, but sold a portion of the site (or 'toft')[3] to Badger for the reconstruction of his premises, and leased the remainder, or part of it, to Johnson for a barn.

Originally the West House may have had a large gable corresponding to that of the East House.[4] The Middle House, with its narrower front, had a 'back' in the rear.

Let us look at the architecture. It is of the homely, substantial type in favour in Warwickshire in the early part of the sixteenth century. A framework of oak rests on a low foundation-wall or 'groundsill', is gripped at each end and consolidated in the centre by massive chimney-stacks, and finally secured by a heavy timber-roof, with thatch, stone, or tile. Workmanship and material are local. Timber is from the Forest, stone from Drayton or other neighbouring quarry, sand from the Gild Pits or Tinkers' Lane, plaster from Welcombe, tile from Warwick. There is no meaningless mixture of geographical incongruities. 'Hard-handed men' were on the spot, who had served their apprenticeship and wore the garb

[1] The generally accepted view is that John occupied the whole block in 1556.   [2] See illustration 28.
[3] A toft is land where once stood a building 'that is fallen or pulled down'.   [4] See illustration 7.

HOUSE FACING THE WEST END OF MIDDLE ROW

(taken down in 1821)

Next to it on our left in Wood Street is a later house with a tall Dutch gable. The little house we see in Henley Street, on our right, is that of William Smith, haberdasher, godfather, as we have supposed, of William Shakespeare

THE BIRTHPLACE IN 1788

(From a sketch made in that year by Col. Phillip De la Motte)

THE BIRTHPLACE. *Restored in 1858*

of their calling—as William Mason, Robert Carpenter, Peter Joiner, Anthony Joiner, John Slater, Richard Tiler. Shakespeare loved them,[1] though he laughed at their drolleries. Sawyers cut the timbers, joiners 'assembled' them, pegging them with wooden nails, laying a lower and stouter story (which was 'close-timbered') on the 'groundsill', and adding the upper (often over-hanging) story (which was 'square-panelled'), then the 'solar' or 'cock-loft' with pointed roof and gables. Slaters or tilers used wooden pegs, or splinters of stagbone, in the roofing, as the carpenters used pegs in the flooring. Spaces between the timbers of the walls were filled with lath and wattle, lath in the 'close-timbered', wattle in the 'square timbered' walling. These were 'daubed' with clay; and when the clay was dry and cracked, it was 'pargetted' (plastered, that is, with a mixture of lime, chalk, ocre, dung or hair), and finished with a thin covering of fine cement.[2] Ground-floors were of clay in a framework of timber, tempered with horse-litter. Masons built the 'groundsill' and the chimneys. The latter rose from a wide open hearth to a heavy shaft, able to resist a storm, and well above the roof to prevent smoking. Iron, what little there is of it, is smith's work, such as Richard Hornby, Richard Goodwin, Edmund Barrett, or John Page would turn out on the anvil, with ease and pleasure—hooks, hinges, latches, the ornamental sign, and weathercock. Locks called for special craft.

Such a dwelling, simple and lasting, full of character, with the mark of the tool and the finger, and therefore pleasure, on every inch of it, was the fitting home of a poet. Given

[1] 'Our artificers were never so excellent as at this present, but their workmanship never less strong and substantial for continuance', says Harrison. Nevertheless, much of it has stood the test of centuries.
[2] One of the new devices was this cement, 'which', says Harrison, 'beside the delectable whiteness of the stuff itself, is laid on so even and smoothly as nothing in my judgement can be done with more exactness'.

imagination it gathers memories and fancies. Shadows and weird noises are in the rafters, the wind is in the chimney, crickets are on the hearth, fairies glisten in the light of the dying fire, through the casement-window shines the moon, from without comes the *to-whit*, *to-whoo* of the owl. Shakespeare's birthplace left its impress deep on his mind and verse. He took it with him to Greenwich Palace and the royal presence in the closing scene of *A Midsummer Night's Dream*.[1]

Let us go in, and look round. We have not John Shakespeare's inventory; but that of his brother alderman, George Whateley, whose house we have mentioned in the same street,[2] is preserved and will serve as a clue to the furniture and other contents of the Poet's house. At Whateley's there was the 'hall',[3] the parlour (a combined sitting and sleeping-room), an inner parlour (the alderman's bed-chamber), a chamber over the 'hall', the 'next chamber', a chamber 'beneath the entry' (next the front-door down the street), the 'maidens' chamber', a kiln-house (for brewing), a 'yeling-house' (for cooling the beer), a buttery and nether-buttery, an apple-chamber, a bolting-house, a garner-house 'next to the garden', a stable (with a roan mare in it), a haybarn, a gate-house at the Gild Pits, and a wood-house. We note painted cloths, cushions, curtains, carpets (for the tables probably), chests, coffers, bedding for six bedsteads, linen, brass, pewter, lead, silver spoons, a salt parcel-gilt, basins of latten, and malt quern, mustard-mill, and candle-mould. There were twenty-two foot of glass in the 'hall', thirty in the parlour, twenty in the chamber over the 'hall'. Other windows had lattice.[4] The alderman had two gowns, a camlet jacket, a cloak, and doublet of Damask.

---

[1] 'Through this Palace with sweet peace, and the Owner of it blest' (v. ii. 48, 50).   [2] p. 15.
[3] The 'hall' was the common living-room.
[4] 'Of old time our country houses instead of glass did use much lattice, and that made either of wicker or fine rifts of oak in checkerwise' (Harrison).

Among his possessions are a bearing-sheet, two fine pillow-biers with bone-lace, two spinning-wheels, two powdering-tubs, nineteen stalls of bees with their hives, and 'wax-honey, and other things in the apple-chamber'.

8. THE BACK

To his father's house in Henley Street, no doubt, William Shakespeare brought his wife from Shottery on his marriage in 1582. It was the custom in Stratford, as elsewhere, for the eldest son to make his home under the parental roof, and if the Poet and his wife lived elsewhere than at the Birthplace before their removal to New Place it was contrary to custom, and we should probably have a hint of it. As with the Dixons, the Parsons', the Smiths, the Hornbys, the Wheelers, the Quyneys, the Sadlers, the Hills', the Rogers', the Reynolds', and almost every family we are acquainted with, two households, we may believe, resided on the Shakespeare premises in Henley Street from 1582 to 1597, and to the end of the Alderman's life.[1] The 'goodman of the house' loved to have his 'many'[2] about him; especially in the night, when, as Harrison tells us,[3] 'lying in his bed' in a central chamber (like the traditional 'Birthroom'), he might 'lightly hear' what was done throughout the building, and 'call quickly' if any danger threatened.

And what part of the building, may we suppose, was allotted to William and Anne, and their children—Susanna and the twins, Hamnet (or Hamlet: the names are identical[4]) and Judith? What but the picturesque 'back', projecting into

[1] The Harts followed the William Shakespeares.
[2] 'meiny', household, as in *King Lear*, II. iv. 35.   [3] ii. 10.
[4] 'Hamlet' and its variants are not uncommon in and around Stratford. I find the following: Elizabeth Hamlets (1543), Amblet (1563), Hamolet Hassall (1564), Hamlet Holdar (1576), Katharine Hamlet (1580), Hamnet Sadler (1580), Hamlet Sadler (1581), Hamnet Shakespeare (1585), Anne Amblar (1596), Hambnet Smith (Aspinall's spelling 1613), Hamlet Smith (1614), and Hamlet Bent (1625).

the garden, which to this day makes an independent little residence. It has its separate kitchen, its separate staircase, and its private entrance; and from its upper story winds a small supplementary stairway into the 'solar' of the front house, affording space there for an additional bed-chamber. In view of the probabilities this conjecture is more than plausible. We may see the attorney's clerk, then the poet and player in his 'native country', as Aubrey tells us, 'once a year',[1] in the garden among the roses and apple-trees, and in his study, overlooking the garden, among books 'prized above a kingdom'. He speaks of the rose more than a hundred times, and specifies eight kinds; he knew a good apple—he names six sorts: the pippin, the bitter-sweeting, the pomewater, the apple-john, the leather-coat. And he knew a good book—his Ovid's *Metamorphoses* from end to end, a constant companion;[2] his Geneva Bible, which he had devoured as a boy, and continued to read, in Beza's 1587 edition,[3] through life; his Puttenham, his Holinshed, his North's *Plutarch's Lives*. His father, we may believe, taught him to read. His father had been Chamberlain, in charge of the borough finances, for three successive years, and I am not aware of a Chamberlain, from first to last, who was not good at figures and able to use his pen. The theory of his illiteracy is, I trust, an exploded fallacy. His series of accounts as Chamberlain exist only in the official copies, but that these *are* copies no one acquainted with the facts can deny. We have but the initials of his ring (I.S.), and his sign-manual—no scrap of writing, so far as we know, from his pen; yet this is true of many others, indeed of the great majority of our Elizabethan Stratford worthies, and it is almost

---

[1] 'He was wont to go to his native country once a year'; and, again, 'was wont to go into Warwickshire once a year' (*Outlines*, ii. 43, 71).
[2] Only those ignorant of Shakespeare, Ovid, or Golding can speak of the Poet's knowledge of Ovid as only or chiefly through Golding's clownish translation (*Minutes and Accounts*, III. xvii–xxvi).
[3] So we conclude from the use of marginalia.

THE BACK (of the Middle House at the Birthplace). Restored in 1858

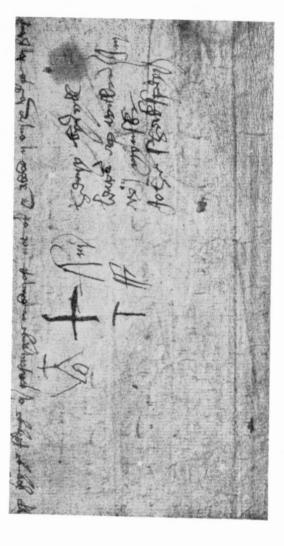

MARKS OF THE AFFEERORS, 4 MAY 1561 (Misc. Doc. vii. 56)

John Shakespeare's Mark, 1561

true of the Stratford Worthiest. Six or seven signatures (four of them containing the interesting dot in the W) is all that remains of the writing of John Shakespeare's famous son. A mark may or may not be evidence of illiteracy. It depends on the mark, which may be a rude cross in a legal document, or an elaborate symbol in a Corporation or 'Brotherhood' record. The plain cross was often employed by educated men. Master Adrian Quyney and Edmund Hathaway (Mistress Shakespeare's nephew) have left us both marks and signatures.[1] Corporation and 'Brotherhood' marks of Shakespeare's childhood and youth have unmistakable affinity with earlier symbolism. Dixon used a Gothic figure *Four*, Whateley (whose signet initials we have[2]) a combined *Alpha* and *Omega* (Revelation i. 8: 'The Beginning and the Ending, saith the Lord'), Cawdrey, as a butcher, a gridiron (probably that of St. Lawrence), Adrian Quyney (who wrote a good business hand: we have five of his letters) an inverted capital Q (or the Hebrew פ?), John Lewis a circle (which may signify the Everlasting), William Tyler (the father of Shakespeare's friend, Richard Tyler) concentric circles and cross (probably a figure representing the Trinity), Richard Boyce and his brother Arthur, tailors, a pair of scissors and a pair of shears, the former a kind of cross, John Taylor, shearman, a pair of calipers, and Lewis ap Williams a church-gable, or something of the kind, with doubtless religious meaning. Best of all is the mark of John

---

[1] Edmund Hathaway witnesses an indenture of 20 Feb. 1620–1 with his mark and a levy by the churchwardens on 10 Aug. 1635 with his signature. Halliwell-Phillipps says, magisterially, 'There is no reasonable pretence for assuming that in the time of John Shakespeare, whatever may have been the case at earlier periods, it was the practice for marks to be used by those who were capable of signing their names' (*Outlines*, ii. 369). A closer study of the Stratford records would have convinced him otherwise. A third example to the contrary is that of Henry Wilson whose mark we have (an inverted V or double VV) and a letter to Richard Quyney (*Master Richard Quyny*, p. 178 f.).
[2] *Halliwell-Phillipps Shakespearean Rarities*, Baker, no. 415.

Shakespeare—a pair of compasses or 'dividers', with a single or a double screw. It is delicately and daintily drawn, evidently by a draughtsman, able to use not only his glover's knife and scissors but his *quill*. I challenge any one but an expert to write it so well.[1] What does it signify? 'God Encompasseth us'?[2] or 'The Measure of my Days, what it is'?[3]

In the 'Back' then, with good reason we may believe, William Shakespeare worked at 'the first heir of his invention' (his first *published* venture), *Venus and Adonis,* and his other early efforts, poetic and dramatic, until under stress of deep emotion, suddenly and magnificently his genius took fire, and he created, as by magic, *King John* and *Romeo and Juliet.* For the first time he *spoke out* in the Bastard, and gave us *moving* tragedy in young Arthur. In perhaps the 'solar' which afforded the additional bed-chamber, died young Hamnet (Hamlet) Shakespeare in August 1596 in his twelfth year.[4] We seem

---

[1] We have three specimens of this beautiful little *signum*, made on 6 Oct. 1559, 4 May 1561, and 27 Sept. 1564. That of 4 May 1561 differs from the other two in being a pair of 'dividers' with parallel legs and double screw.

[2] This was a puritan motto (cf. Psalm xxxii. 10: 'He that trusteth in the Lord, mercy shall compass him', Geneva Version), supposed to be the origin of the sign, 'Goat and Compasses'.

[3] Psalm xxxix. 4 (Geneva Version).

[4] He was baptized 2 Feb. 1585 and buried 11 Aug. 1596. *King John* and *Romeo and Juliet* were written, there is every reason to believe, in the late summer and autumn of 1596. To date the latter play, or any part of it, 1591, on a supposed *literal* allusion in the Nurse's speech, I. iii. 16–35, to the Earthquake of 1580, is to throw dramatic and literary criticism to the winds. The essential part of the speech is the emphasis pointedly on Juliet's extreme youth. Shakespeare dramatically and represents her as *fourteen* (not sixteen, as in his original, Arthur Brooke's *Romeus and Juliet,* l. 1,846): whence the period since her weening and the episode in the orchard has to be *eleven.* Had Shakespeare (following Brooke) made her sixteen (which was too old for her girlish irresponsibility), the interval would have been *thirteen years* (and the date of the play 1593!). Shakespeare could not have written the Nurse's speech, with its disconnected chatter and jerky metre (mid-verse pauses and eleventh syllables), in 1591 (nor 1593).

(Signatures and marks attached to the Resolution of 27 Sept. 1564 by the Borough Council. Council Book, A, 5)

JOHN SHAKESPEARE'S MARK, 1564

THE HIGH CROSS

(as drawn by Saunders before it was taken down in 1831)

We look from the High Street, across the top of Middle Row on our right, to the house on the sites of Ainge's shop and the Angel in Back Bridge Street. Middle Row has lost 'The Corner Shop' and 'Bott's Shop' in its rear, the sites of which have been thrown into the Market Place. We recognize the tall shop and Burbage's Tavern, as in Grubb's painting of 1769

CORNER OF HIGH STREET AND WOOD STREET IN 1835
AFTER THE REMOVAL OF THE CROSS

(after a drawing by Mrs. E. F. Flower)

The Hill-Sturley houses, with the gatehouse, appear on the right (nos. 4–6). Here Shakespeare may have worked as an attorney's clerk

to see and hear the distressed mother in the heart-rending
lines:

> Grief fills the room up of my absent child,
> Lies in his bed, walks up and down with me,
> Puts on his pretty looks, repeats his words,
> Remembers me of all his gracious parts,
> Stuffs out his vacant garments with his form.[1]

If Arthur's death is the first really tragic thing in Shakespeare, the death of Mercutio is the second, and the suicide of
the lovers is the third. Only pedantry detects the apprentice
hand in *Romeo and Juliet*. From first to last it is a masterpiece,
a finished work of art; and not the least masterly feature is the
swift development of the hero from a sonnet-fancied youth
into a desperate man—the transformation of his languid,
amorous vapourings into short, sharp sentences that burst
from him like pistol-shots. This convulsive change of senti-
ment into passion is a revelation of the Poet's heart.[2]

9. THE HIGH CROSS

LET us follow John Shakespeare on market day (which was
Thursday) from Henley Street, past a picturesque timber
house facing the west-end of Middle Row,[3] to his standing at
the Cross, and while he is disposing of his handwear among
his customers, look round at the place and the people. The
Cross, or rather 'the High Cross House', to give it its full title,
was a quaint structure of timber and plaster, erected four-
square on stout wooden pillars above the ancient, now or
later headless, stone shaft. The roof was surmounted by a
turret which held the clock; which clock had one face or dial

---

[1] *King John*, III. iv. 93–7.
[2] Compare v. i. 24–6, 29–36, 58–60, 83–6; v. iii. 22–7, 60–7 with
I. i. 177–200, 214–44, and other *purposely* sentimental passages in light
verse. To describe these as early style is only true to the extent that
they are in the Poet's earlier manner—to which he reverts to mark
Romeo's juvenile temper prior to his meeting Juliet.
[3] It connected Henley Street with Wood Street. See Illustration 6.

with a single hand of gilded bronze. The floor of the 'house' projected some feet beyond the walls, providing cover for the glovers and a ledge for performers or spectators at a festival. Suspended beneath the floor were leather fire-buckets, a fire-hook, and a ladder. Stairs led through a trap-door into the chamber, which was the domain of the clock-setter, the in-offensive and beloved curate, Sir William Gilbert *alias* Higgës. The town was all alive to-day and on fair-days. Cattle were on sale in Rother Market, pigs in Swine (Ely) Street, sheep in Sheep Street, horses in the Church Way. Corn-wains were unloaded in Corn Street, salt-wains at the Cross in Rother Market; timber was piled in Wood Street; sellers of hides had their station at the Cross in Rother Market, pewterers and bedders in Wood Street, braziers in Bridge Street, ironmongers in Bridge Street, nailers opposite the *Angel*, collar-makers and ropers in Bridge Street, salters and sugarers in Corn Street, purveyors of white meat (butter, cheese, eggs), of wick yarn (for candles), and of fruit, at the Chapel or White Cross, tanners in the Gild Hall (beneath the School) where the 'sealers' marked the leather, fleshers at the top of Middle Row, and poulterers elsewhere. But the High Cross was the chief centre of activity and authority. Here was the Whipping-post [1] for rogues, vagabonds, and prostitutes. 'I had as lief be whipped', says Gremio, 'at the High Cross every morning'; [2] whence we conclude that offenders after a night in gaol began their day with salutory castigation at the hands of the Beadle— Newall, Meekins, or John Hemmings. The 'Gaol' was in High Street (just below the disused *Cage* and, as said before, not to be confused with it), and in its vicinity was the Ducking-stool (when not at the riverside) for fraudulent traders and scolds; also the Stocks (unless this was in the Corn Market at Sheep Street) for drunkards (like Sly), [3] swearers, abusive and violent persons, and other mean delinquents. We remember Lear's

[1] Council Book B, p. 262.   [2] *Taming of the Shrew*, I.i. 137.   [3] *Ib.* Ind. i. 2.

wrath at the stocking of his messenger[1]—it was a very great indignity. The Pillory was in the Corn Market,[2] for thieves. 'I stood as on a pillory', says Hortensio, 'looking through the lute.'[3] Launce both stood on the pillory and sat in the stocks for the misbehaviour of his dog, Crab.[4] Within the Gaol were branding-irons for sheep-stealers. Belief in the efficacy of public ignominy was an article of the Elizabethan Calvinistic creed.

Where the crowd was, John Taborer[5] would be, a Stratford musician, playing lively music on his drum and pipe; or Thomas Clarke taborer,[6] who got into trouble for playing in time of divine service;[7] or John Knowles 'minstrel';[8] or the blind harper young Philip Sidney heard with emotion at Chipping Norton, singing the old ballad of Percy and Douglas, a man who had made his way, with kindly help, in the livery of his master, Sir William Holles, from Nottinghamshire.[9] In the crowd, selling her wares, was a female Autolycus, one Avice Clarke, who was well known in Stratford and died there, leaving the residue of her small belongings to her executor, Robert Johnson of Henley Street. In her pedlar's pack were quoifs of black and tawney and 'drawn work'; handkerchiefs and crest-cloths, bands, garters, gloves, cross-gartering, laces, points, white 'inkle' or tape, loom-work, thread, bandstrings, hand-carved buttons, pins, brooches, boxes, thimbles, 'bound graces', 42 yards of bone-lace, 4½ dozen yards of loom-work lace, and shreds of lace and calico, valued altogether at 47s.: say £30 in our money.[10] These simple, hand-made things would be worth very much more to-day. We should have to ransack our shops, full of machine-made wares, for their artistic equivalents.

[1] *King Lear*, II. iv. 12–27.   [2] *Muniments*, 255, 370, 495.
[3] *Tam. Shrew*, II. i. 157.   [4] *Two Gent.* IV. iv. 33–6.
[5] *Minutes and Accounts*, iii. 82 (one of the trained band in 1580).
[6] A later comer, who survived Shakespeare.   [7] In 1621.
[8] Living in 1574.   [9] *Sidney*, Wallace, pp. 65 f., 421.
[10] *Wills and Inventories*, 19; *Misc. Doc.* i. 83, xiii. 65.

10. MASTER NICHOLAS LANE

ONE frequenter of the Stratford market we may see in effigy on his gravestone at Alveston. This was Master Nicholas Lane of Bridge Town. The Lanes, like the Shakespeares, rose from yeomen to be 'gentlemen'. Old Richard Lane, 'Goodman Lane', knew John Shakespeare, and appreciated his ability, appointing him his lay-attorney in a suit in the Court of Record in 1556. Nicholas Lane, old Richard's son, prospered as a farmer, and as a money-lender, and became Master Lane of Bridge Town. Once at least he had the honour of being appointed on a commission with Sir Thomas Lucy,[1] and he contributed with a neighbour[2] the cost of a light horseman to Tilbury against the Spaniards in 1588. But he is chiefly remembered for a suit against John Shakespeare, as surety for a loan to Henry Shakespeare, John's brother, a farmer at Ingon. John denied the responsibility, resisted the suit through all stages, and when judgement was given against him, appealed to a higher court.[3] Lane also was determined. He was capable at times of personal violence. He was fined in 1592 for assaulting one Francis Jackman of Henley-in-Arden with a crab-tree cudgel, and wounding him so seriously that for a time his life was despaired of.[4] Lane died in 1595. The 'tomb-maker' has not flattered him. I do not believe that John Shakespeare's fierce antagonist had quite such a receding chin as he has given him. The block of stone has had to do with it. But the garments are trustworthy—a leather (?) doublet buttoned up the front, with sleeves buttoned on the shoulders and up their sides, knee-breeches pleated in front, with pockets, and embroidered at the sides with rosettes, worsted stockings (probably the yellow worsted in fashion in Warwickshire and

[1] In the case of Alice Browne, 1587.
[2] Edmund Pearse of Alveston.
[3] Court of Record Jan.–Mar. 1587.
[4] *Records of Henley* (Wellstood), p. 33.

MASTER NICHOLAS LANE, 1595

HOUSE OF THE OLD TYPE IN THE ROTHER STREET

Notice the horizontal hanging shutters, which did service before the windows were glazed, and also provided when half raised a projecting shelf for the display of shop goods. The brick-work between the timbers has replaced the old wattle and daub, and distorted the framework

worn by Sir Fulke Greville's retainers), shoes the thongs of
which are tied with a thick lace in a bow, ruffs at the neck and
wrists, and a belt from which is suspended a short sword.

His brother, John Lane, had a taste for fine clothes. John
held to the Old Faith, was presented in 1592 with the Cloptons,
Reynolds' and other Romanists who paid their monthly fine
for absence from church. On Monday 5 November 1593
he ordered of William Hiccocks, the Catholic tailor in Wood
Street,[1] a pair of hose buff, a pair of hose laced with green lace,
a pair of hose laced with black lace, a pair of Venetian hose
laced with blue lace, and a jerkin of frieze. The previous
month he ordered a cloak, for which Hiccocks purchased
skeins of silk.[2] Stratford, if at this time a puritan stronghold,
did not lack splashes of colour in the streets. We read of a
Jesuit priest running for life in Chapel Street, or the Old Town,
one day in January 1604, disguised in green 'round hose', white
stockings, and high-heeled shoes. He fell, poor fellow, in the
mud, threatened to overthrow a boy in his path, and found
refuge at last in the house of Master Thomas Reynolds. The
Town Clerk was eager to capture him, Shakespeare's kinsman
and fellow resident at New Place, Master Thomas Greene;[3]
his protector was the father of Shakespeare's friend (to whom
he left a gold memorial ring), William Reynolds. Amid such
conflicting creeds and passions did the Poet, the greatest
peacemaker of his time, live and do his beautiful work.

11. HIGH STREET

WE are still in the middle of the town. Interesting folk,
well known to Shakespeare, are all about us, grave
burghers busy in their occupations, keen about religion, state
affairs, and, be it noted, education. In Wood Street was

---

[1] On the site of no. 44.   [2] Misc. Doc. iii. 129.
[3] *Ib.* xii. 72.

William Parsons,[1] friend of Walter Roche the Schoolmaster,[2] and kinsman, by his marriage, of Hamlet Sadler. He and his wife, Margaret Sadler, may have been close friends of their neighbours in Henley Street, the Shakespeares.[3] He prospered as a draper, was prominent in the Corporation, rebuilt his house after the fire of 1594, and sent his son John (possibly John Shakespeare's godson) to Balliol College in 1597. Also in Wood Street [4] lived the lawyer and Latinist, a Cambridge scholar and pronounced puritan, evidently an admirer at Cambridge (1569–70) of Thomas Cartwright, Abraham Sturley. He succeeded his father-in-law Richard Hill, in the house, and rebuilt it after the fire of 1594. He was legal agent with Henry Rogers, the Town Clerk, to Sir Thomas Lucy. He sent two sons to Oxford, Henry to Exeter, Richard to Balliol.[5] At the Corner House in Middle Row, facing the Market Cross, lived Francis Smith, haberdasher and 'gentleman', eldest son of Shakespeare's godfather (as I have presumed) in Henley Street.[6] He left money for the 'schooling', that is, University training,[7] of a godson and nephew. He bequeathed, too, £10 to a student at Oxford, the son of his neighbour in the High Street, William Chandler.[8] In the High Street were a score of able men worthy of Shakespeare's acquaintance and friendship. We must note Daniel Baker,[9] kinsman of Abraham Sturley, and, like him, a pronounced puritan. He disliked plays, of the type, at any rate, coming into fashion at the close of Elizabeth's reign ('far unlike the plays and harmless morals of former times', as a Gloucestershire squire lamented),[10] and when Bailiff in 1603 he obtained

---

[1] Nos. 26–8.   [2] p. 48.
[3] *Master Richard Quyny*, pp. 39–41.   [4] Nos. 4–6.
[5] They entered the Church, and became 'minister of Broadway' and 'minister of Alcester'.   [6] p. 15.   [7] *Hamlet*, I. ii. 113.
[8] p. 33 f.   [9] p. 70 f.
[10] Robert Willis, in his *Mount Tabor or Private Exercises of a Penitent Sinner*, 1639. He tells how profoundly moved he was as a boy, some

the prohibition of performances by travelling players in the Gild Hall.[1] His son, Daniel, matriculated at Oxford the following year. We must note William Walford, and the handsome house he built,[2] a few doors below Daniel Baker's, after the fire of 1595. At the corner of High Street and Sheep Street was the house,[3] rebuilt after this fire, of Hamlet Sadler and his wife Judith, the godparents probably of Shakespeare's twin-children, Hamlet and Judith, baptized in 1585. Opposite in the High Street were the fine houses (still standing) of the new order (of the old type but larger, of three stories with carvings) erected after the same fire by John Wilmore (the so-called 'Tudor House'),[4] William and Roger Smith (now the Garrick Inn), and Thomas Rogers (the misnamed 'Harvard House'). William and Roger Smith were brothers of Francis Smith of the 'Corner House' above. William Smith and John Wilmore married daughters of Thomas Rogers, and their houses may owe something to the instigation and wealth of their father-in-law, who was a butcher, and a man of character as well as of means. A third daughter of Thomas Rogers, by a younger wife, married Robert Harvard of Southwark in 1605, and became the mother in 1607 of John Harvard, the founder of Harvard University. Her name was Katharine. Higher up the street were the shops of William Chandler[5] and Alderman William Smith,[6] the tavern [7] of Thomas Atwood

seventy years before, by a morality play given by travelling actors in Gloucester and laments the degradation of the drama since.

[1] The year of this prohibition was remembered as 'Master Baker's year'. William Chandler when Bailiff in 1617–18 broke the order (which had been renewed in 1612) and directed the Chamberlain (who was Shakespeare's nephew, Richard Hathaway) to pay 5s. to a company of players, and 3s. 6d. to a company that came with a show to the Town.   [2] Nos. 17 and 18.

[3] Where the Corn-Exchange now stands.

[4] Wilmore's house has been disfigured by the enlargement of the top, gabled, story.

[5] p. 32. His house was on the site of no. 31.

[6] On the site of no. 33 or 35.   [7] On the site of no. 36.

alias Taylor (who was a friend of Richard Shakespeare, the
Poet's grandfather) and his successors (including John Smith
the vintner, brother of Francis, William, and Roger, and probably godson of John Shakespeare), and the shop and dwelling [1]
of Adrian Quyney and his son Richard. William Chandler,
father of the boy at Oxford the beneficiary of Francis Smith,
was stepson of Shakespeare's cousin, Thomas Greene, and his
enthusiastic supporter against the younger Combes.[2] Alderman William Smith (to be distinguished from his namesake the
haberdasher in Henley Street) was a wealthy mercer, brother-
in-law to John Watson, Fellow of All Souls, Oxford, and
Bishop of Winchester. The first Protestant vicar of Stratford,
John Bretchgirdle, M.A. of Oxford, was tutor to Alderman
Smith's children. On his death (probably from the effects of
the terrible plague of 1564) he bequeathed them books, including a Sallust, a Justin, Tully's Offices, a Horace, a Virgil,
and copies of a favourite and characteristic volume, Tye's
Acts of the Apostles in English Metre for the Lute.

Of the friendship and correspondence of Abraham Sturley
and his 'brother in the Lord', Richard Quyney, I have written
in my little book *Master Richard Quyny.* Sturley wrote Latin,
and Quyney at least read Latin, as easily almost as English.
A charming letter is extant in Latin to Quyney from his
eleven-year-old boy, presumably at the Grammar School.
It must be given as an example of what a grocer's boy could
do in Stratford at that age. The brother referred to, as also
in need of a writing-book, was probably Thomas, aged nine
and a half, who was a good penman. He married Shakespeare's younger daughter, Judith.[3] Here is the letter:

Patri suo amantissimo Mro.[4] Richardo Quinye
Richardus Quinye filius S.P.D.[5]
Ego omni officio ac potius pietate erga te (mi pater) tibi gratias

[1] On the site of no. 37.   [2] p. 65 f.
[3] See p. 78.   [4] Magistro.   [5] Salutem Plurimam Dicit.

ago iis omnibus beneficiis quæ in me contulisti; te etiam oro et
obsecro ut provideres fratri meo et mihi duos chartaceos
libellos quibus maxime caremus hoc presenti tempore; si enim
eos haberemus, plurimus profecto iis usus esset nobis; et præ-
terea gratias tibi ago quia a teneris, quod aiunt, unguiculis,[1]
educasti me in sacræ doctrinæ studiis usque ad hunc diem: Absit
etiam verbulis meis vana adulationis suspicio, neque enim quen-
quam ex meis amicis cariorem aut amantiorem mei te esse judico,
et vehementer obsecro ut maneat semper egregius iste amor
tuus sicut semper antehac, et quanquam ego non possum re-
munerare tua beneficia, omnem tamen ab intimis meis præcor-
diis tibi exoptabo salutem: Vale.

Filiolus tuus tibi obedientissimus

Richardus Quinye.[2]

We may translate thus:

To his most loving father, Master Richard Quinye,
Richard Quinye the son bids very good health.

With all respect, nay, rather with filial affection towards thee,
my father, I give thee thanks for all those kindnesses which thou
hast bestowed upon me; also I pray and beseech thee that thou
wouldst provide for my brother and me two paper books, which
we very much want at this present time; for if we had them we
should truly find great use for them; and moreover, I give thee
thanks that 'from tender soft nails', as they say, unto this day[3]
thou hast instructed me in the studies of Sacred Learning.
Far from my poor words be even a suspicion of flattery, for I
deem not any one of my friends to be dearer or more loving of
me than thou art, and earnestly I pray that that surpassing love
of thine may always remain as always hitherto; and although I
am not able to repay thy kindnesses, nevertheless I shall wish
thee from my heart of hearts all prosperity. Farewell.

Thy little son most obedient unto thee

Richard Quinye.

[1] Cicero, *Epistolae ad Familiares*, i. 6. 2.
[2] Malone, ii. 564.   [3] About 5 Oct. 1598.

Quyney died, as I have learnt since I wrote his Life, of a wound received in the performance of his duty as Bailiff in 1602. He was hurt, accidentally and fatally, by one of his servants in suppressing a brawl in the town by followers of the oppressive and probably crazy lord of the manor, Sir Edward Greville.

In High Street lived Shakespeare's friend Henry Walker, and Philip Rogers the apothecary.

Henry Walker may have been a grandson, or other kinsman, of Henry Walker (Walker, Wager) of Snitterfield, whose will was witnessed by the Poet's grandfather, Richard Shakespeare, in 1558.[1] He was a mercer in Stratford, married to a wife Dorothy, with a son John newly born, when he witnessed John Shakespeare's conveyance of a strip of his 'toft' to George Badger in Henley Street in January 1597.[2] He prospered in business, became 'gentleman', and churchwarden, served as a burgess, chamberlain, and alderman in the Corporation, and was three times bailiff, in 1607-8, 1624-5, 1635-6. His brother-in-law, John Smith the ironmonger (son of William the Alderman), disliked him, otherwise he was a favourite. His son, William, by a second wife, baptized on Sunday 16 October 1608, had Shakespeare for godfather. Shakespeare left the boy a gold piece of 20s. in 1616.[3] Henry Walker was a leader in the defence of borough rights against Sir Edward Greville,[4] and in his old age, at Michaelmas 1638, was appointed on a deputation to London to treat with the Earl of Middlesex about the unhappy differences between the Corporation and the vicar, Doctor Hall's friend, Thomas Wilson.[5]

Philip Rogers the apothecary is noteworthy. He sold confections of roses, liquorice, aniseed, sarsaparilla, sassafras, hermodactilis, pills, cassia fistula, mastic, oil of vitriol, Venice

---

[1] 'Among the Shakespeare Archives' (*Notes and Queries*, Oct. 1920–Apr. 1921).   [2] p. 20.
[3] 'to my godson William Walker xxˢ. in gold.'
[4] *Master Richard Quyny*, pp. 171, 175.   [5] Council Book C., p. 164.

turpentine, guaiacum wood and bark, Burgundy pitch, precipitate cinnabar, corrosive sublimate, diagredium, and other concoctions calculated to disturb and agitate the inside. Men's lives in those days were sometimes saved, if they survived it, by 'evacuation'. Rogers also sold the drug which old Quyney called 'tobecka', and against which Sturley warned Richard Quyney.[1] He sold, moreover, clay-pipes, some nine inches long, with small economical bowls, flat bottomed to rest, between well-inhaled puffs, upon a table. Last but not least, he sold ale. A patient, therefore, feeling sore after a dose of diagredium or corrosive sublimate, might purchase consolation on the premises. His pipe and a modicum of the soothing weed (*quaedam parcella tobacci et una pipa*) would cost him threepence.[2]

Needy as Philip Rogers certainly was (we are not told that he went 'in tattered weeds, with overwhelming brows'),[3] he sent a son to Oxford, who obtained his licence to practise surgery.[4]

12. SHEEP STREET

IN Sheep Street were other interesting neighbours. George Badger, owner of the house next door to John Shakespeare in Henley Street, had his shop and dwelling next door to Hamlet Sadler below the Pillory. He was brother by baptism of Richard Quyney (his father, Thomas Badger, the wealthy miller of Bidford Grange, was Richard Quyney's godfather), a woollen-draper, with considerable property and many children, and staunch Catholic convictions. He was a rebel in his puritan environment, paid fines and went to prison for his recusancy, refused to obey orders at meetings of the Corporation and was deprived of his alderman's gown, har-

[1] *Master Richard Quyny*, pp. 136 f., 147, 152.
[2] Court of Record Manuscripts, iii. 314; Misc. Doc. xii. 95. Unfortunately Romeo did not obtain this comfort in Verona, or he might have kept the deadly 'compound' for which he paid 'forty ducats' in his pocket.   [3] *Romeo and Juliet*, v. i. 39.
[4] *Athenae*, Wood. *Register of the University*, ii. I, 125.

boured 'massing relics' from Clopton in the time of Gunpowder Plot, and ten years afterwards had his house searched
by candlelight (at a cost of 2*d*. for candles to the Borough
Chamberlain). Older than Shakespeare he survived him nearly
twenty years. Just below Badger in Sheep Street lived his rival
woollen-draper (wool in all forms was a source of wealth in
Stratford), an uncompromising puritan, John Shakespeare's
fellow recusant, Nicholas Barnhurst. Badger was his *bête noire*.
He lost his temper with him at the Council meetings, called
him 'knave' and 'rascal' and had to apologize, on another occasion abused others besides Badger and 'the whole Company',
and was 'removed', otherwise 'expulsed' as an alderman.

Both Badger and Barnhurst suffered severely in the fire
of 1595. So did William Rogers, a Serjeant at the Mace,
brother-in-law of Shakespeare's friend, Henry Walker. He
was in office when Shakespeare drew his delightful burlesque
of a serjeant in *The Comedy of Errors* in 1592.[1] In his 'boots'[2]
and 'suit' of 'buff' (light yellow leather), carrying the town-
mace, as the symbol of his authority to distrain or arrest, he
was a conspicuous and somewhat awe-inspiring person. His
dwelling, the old 'Shrieve's House',[3] a few doors below Barnhurst's, he reconstructed and enlarged, converting part of it
into a tavern for the sale of *aqua vitae*, balm water, and *rosa
salis*, with aniseed and liquorice, as well as ale. For the distilla-
tion of spirits he kept 'two limbecs and a still'. After his death
in 1597, his widow Elizabeth, *née* Walker, kept the house
(which had much glass in the windows) and tavern, and prospered. Her daughter, Elizabeth, married a 'gentleman',
Master Matthew Morris, a friend of Shakespeare's daughter,
Susanna, and her husband, Doctor John Hall. If the Poet was
in Stratford he probably attended the marriage, and the 'good

[1] IV. i and IV. ii. 31–62. Something from London (the Counter prison)
is in the representation.
[2] *Minutes and Accounts*, ii. 49 ('a pair of boots for Russell 5*s*.')   [3] No. 40.

HOUSES OF THE NEW TYPE

25, 26 High Street

(Rogers, Smith, Wilmore)

'THE SHRIEVE'S HOUSE'

(40 *Sheep Street*)

Rebuilt after the Fire of 1595 by William Rogers, Sergeant-at-the-Mace, and his wife, Elizabeth Walker, sister to Shakespeare's friend, Henry Walker. Here the Poet probably attended the wedding feast of their daughter Elizabeth and Master Matthew Morris on Wednesday 13 Oct. 1613

man's feast' at the house after it, on Wednesday 13 October 1613. Master Morris went to live with his wife at the house, and here no doubt their children were born, whose names are significant of friendship with the Halls at New Place—Susanna in August 1614, again Susanna in November 1616, Elizabeth in September 1618, and John in December 1620. Save the Birthplace no dwelling in Stratford is more precious.

Three doors from the 'Shrieve's House' was the dwelling [1] of John Shakespeare's old colleague, John Taylor the shearman, nine years a Chamberlain of the Borough. His premises stretched to the back of the *Bear*, where he had a barn. He left Stratford in 1592.

Opposite lived William Wyatt and the Tylers. Wyatt was bailiff in Gunpowder-Plot time, and made a memorable raid on Clopton House, in the tenure of Ambrose Rookwood the conspirator, on 6 November 1605, carrying off chalices, crucifixes, crosses, vestments, pictures, Latin prayer-books, beads, a pax, and other damning evidence of 'papistry'.[2] The same day he bought up gunpowder and shot in the town. Popular feeling actively supported him and the Deputy Lieutenant, old Fulke Greville.

Richard Tyler, son of John Shakespeare's colleague in the Chamberlainship, William Tyler, was William Shakespeare's friend, two years and five months his junior, probably a younger schoolfellow. He wore his sword and dagger as a recruit against the Armada in the summer of 1588, and, aged twenty-two, won the heart of Master Richard Woodward's eldest daughter at Shottery Manor, aged about sixteen, whom he married, apparently in secret, to the indignation of her people, especially of her wealthy grandfather, old Robert Perrott, the puritan brewer, owner of 'King's House' (or 'Hall')[3]

---

[1] No. 37.   [2] Inquisition 26 Feb. 1606. *Birthplace Catalogue*, p. 9.
[3] 'my messuage or tenement situate in Stratford known and commonly called by the name of King's Hall or King's House.'

in Stratford (the tavern in Rother Market with mural paintings of Tobias [1]) and the adjoining messuage at the corner of Rother Market and Windsor,[2] with an orchard which ran back to the gardens in Henley Street, as well as the Vicarage in Church Street. Perrott, who died shortly after the marriage, at his country-house in Nether Quinton, cut her off in his will (8 March 1589),[3] with stern warning to her sisters to be 'dutiful and obedient' and not to 'match themselves' without the 'consent of their parents'. Young Tyler, whose wedding might have contributed matter to *Romeo and Juliet* (Perrott had something of Capulet in him), had sympathy from his father's colleagues on the Council, who elected him a burgess in 1590. Good Richard Hill, in his will of this year, left him 40s. as his 'cousin'.[4] Shakespeare may have stood godfather to his child, William, baptized on Sunday 9 July 1598. He lived to be a credit to his friends (though he did not stay long in the Council), a well-to-do and honoured 'gentleman'. He outlived Shakespeare (who left him 26s. 8d. for a memorial ring in 1616) twenty years, dying aged seventy in December 1636.

13. CHAPEL STREET

RETRACING our steps we are in Chapel Street (also called Corn Street), facing the Chapel, with the house of William Walker on our left (the corner house of Chapel Street and Sheep Street), and that of Richard Symons (the corner house of Chapel Street and Swine Street, otherwise Ely Street) on our right. Of Walker we know little save that he was a tanner (not to be confused with his namesake in Henley Street a farrier and *equarius medicus*), served as chamberlain and churchwarden, gained gentlehood, and sold his house to the Corporation for the site of a 'Market House' or Town Hall.

[1] Kept by Robert Perrott's brother William in 1564. See p. 3.
[2] 'My messuage in Stratford there called the Rodder or Beast Market.'
[3] P. C. C. 39 Leicester.
[4] By Perrott's marriage with Abraham Sturley's mother in 1572.

This site was part of the estate of Sir Hugh Clopton in 1497. Of Richard Symons we know a good deal, though he belonged to an earlier generation. Shakespeare may have remembered him (his father knew him well), for he was Town Clerk from about 1534 to 1569 and died a few weeks before Shakespeare went to the Grammar School.[1] He was a 'character', master of his legal Latin, writer of a multitude of borough documents in a fine Gothic hand, an autocratic, dignified old fellow who would not be 'thou'-ed, slandered, or assailed by any one, even Robert Perrott, with impunity. Proudly he wrote himself, *verus et fidelis legeus Domine Regine et sic apud omnes graves homines et fideles subditos eiusdem Regine a tempore nativitatis suae et ita inter omnes notos et vicinos suos acceptus datus et reputatus.*[2]

Next door to Walker's were the dwelling and 'Wool House' of Hugh Reynolds, a well-to-do and well-connected yeoman. His wife was Joyce, daughter to Walter Blount of Glason Park. He owned leases of 'Colles' (Colley's?) Farm in Old Stratford, a farm at Shottery, and 'Hall's Close' by the Bridge, and was owner or lessee of at least seven barns—three in Swine Street, one on Bankcroft Side, one in Chapel Lane, the Old Town Barn, and the College Tithe-Barn. His house in Chapel Street was of modest dimensions but very comfortably furnished, of two stories, containing a 'hall', a parlour, two upper chambers, a servants' chamber, a kitchen and buttery. The 'Wool House' held ten tod of wool, valued at £10. On the farms were 240 sheep, valued at £30, 8 oxen, 5 cows, 2 steers, a bull, 6 cart-horses, more horses (including a 'best gelding') and swine. Seventy-six quarters of grain and peas were stored in the barns. Hugh Reynolds died in 1556. His son, Thomas, who married Margaret, the daughter and coheiress to William Gower of Redmarley, and had by her a large family, made his home, in

[1] If he went to school at the regulation age of seven years.
[2] 'Among the Shakespeare Archives' (*Notes and Queries*, 29 Jan. 1921).

or before 1585, at Colles (Colley's?) Farm near the Church. His household in 1595 consisted, with servants, of no less than twenty-two persons, and was the largest we hear of in Stratford. He and his wife were stout Roman Catholics, paying their monthly fines for recusancy. Their eldest son, the heir of his mother, William, born in 1575, was one of the numerous young men of good family who enjoyed the friendship of Shakespeare. He married a lady from London, Frances de Bois, at Clifford Chambers, on 3 August 1615. Shakespeare may have been at the wedding. 'To William Reynolds gentleman' he left in his will, in March 1616, '26s. 8d. to buy him a ring.'

Symons' house (which passed to Francis Burnell, a tailor) was burned down in the fire of 1595; as was the office, an old gate-house, of William Court the lawyer, lower down the street on the same side. The other side escaped this con-flagration, but suffered (at least did the upper end of it) when the Cavaliers, in temporary occupation, to retaliate on Lord Brooke in their retreat, blew up the new Town Hall in 1643. It was 'torn in pieces', with damage doubtless to adjoining property. After this, we may conclude, the handsome five-gabled timber building of the new type which is now part of the 'Shakespeare Hotel', was erected on the ground of the Reynolds messuage and wool-house and a tenement below.[1]

14. NEW PLACE

At the corner of Chapel Street, parted from the Chapel by a lane (down which ran the 'mere' to a 'walk-mill' by the Avon in the tenure of the Sadlers, whence it was known as 'Walkers' Street') stood 'New Place'. The Chapel and 'New Place' must ever be associated. They were built by the same man, the munificent builder of the Bridge, Sir Hugh Clopton, the Chapel to say his prayers in, 'New Place' to end his days in, though he said his last prayers and died in London. The

[1] There is no reason for identifying this handsome building with New Place (H. E. Forrest, *Old Houses in Stratford on Avon*, pp. 93–107).

THE GILD CHAPEL

The tower, nave, and porch rebuilt by Sir Hugh Clopton in 1496–7. The chancel built in 1451–2. To the right is the Gild Hall, and beyond it the Almshouse. On our left is the site of New Place

THE GILD CHAPEL (*restored*)

garden-entrance faced the Chapel.[1] Leland wrote in 1542 of the 'right goodly Chapel' and 'the pretty house of brick-and-timber by the north side of it'. In 1532,[2] and probably from the first, the house was called 'New Place'. It had been built in a new style (which was not followed by Thomas Rogers), brick being substituted, with rather disastrous consequences (as the history of the house proves), for the light wattle-and-plaster between the timbers. Clopton called it his 'great house',[3] in contra-distinction to lesser dwellings on his estate, as at the corners of High Street and Swine Street (afterwards Wilmore's) and Chapel Street and Sheep Street (afterwards Walker's).[4] It had a frontage of 60 feet, a breadth in one place of 70, and was 28 feet high. It contained not less than ten rooms with a hearth.[5] For some years it was occupied by a distinguished retired physician, Doctor Thomas Bentley, who took pleasure in farming and his fine collection of silver, gifts probably of Court patients.[6] He left the house in 1549 'in great ruin and decay'; which is evidence, in a building only half a century old, of the defective structure. Early in Elizabeth's reign it passed mysteriously into the possession of the Clopton's unscrupulous agent, William Bott, whose place as alderman on his expulsion from the Corporation was taken by Shakespeare's father.[7] Bott probably took advantage of young Clopton's difficulties and fears as a Catholic. From Bott the house was purchased by a rival lawyer, William Underhill of Idlicote,[8] whose son

[1] 'To the best of his remembrance, there was a brick wall next the street, with a kind of porch at that end of it near the Chapel' (Richard Grimmitt to Joseph Greene, 24 Oct. 1767, *Outlines*, ii. 134).
[2] Indenture between William Clopton and Elizabeth Cole his sister for her marriage money charged on 'a messuage called the New Place', 20 July, 24 Hen. VIII (*Shakespearean Rarities*, no. 145).
[3] In his will 14 Sept. 1498 (P. C. C. 2 Horne).
[4] Inquisitio p. m., 1 Nov. 1497.   [5] *Outlines*, ii. 110.
[6] 'Among the Shakespeare Archives' (*Notes and Queries*, Oct. 1920.)
[7] *Minutes and Accounts*, I. lvii–lx. Conveyance of 20 Feb. 1563 (*Shakespearean Rarities*, no. 143). Indenture 20 Dec. 1563 (*ib*. 144).
[8] Indenture 1 Sept. 1567 (*ib*. 146).

sold it in 1597 to Shakespeare. Houses were scarce after the fires of 1594 and 1595, and Shakespeare paid a high price, altogether £120 for the property, which consisted of a barn-yard and two barns, two gardens and two orchards, besides the messuage. He spent also on reparations.[1] For the first and only time he shows an interest in architecture (or rather, building operations) in one of the earliest plays written at New Place—*The Second Part of King Henry the Fourth*:

> When we mean to build,
> We first survey the plot, then draw the model;
> And when we see the figure of the house,
> Then must we rate the cost of the erection;

and a dozen and a half lines more.[2] He betrays on this subject none of the persistent and technical acquaintance he manifests in country-town law.

The neighbourhood was pleasant[3] and peaceful. On Shake-speare's side of the lane beyond his garden, which became known as his 'Great Garden', were barns and elms—his own barn and some half a dozen more: examples, as Halliwell-Phillipps well says, 'of the store-houses for corn so numerous before the enclosure of the common lands'. On the Chapel side, beyond the Chapel, was the 'Gild Garden', within its picturesque 'mud-wall', containing an orchard and bowling-green, a dovehouse, an herbarium and fountain, a walnut-tree and crab-tree seats; and beyond it were cottages (one of which was Shakespeare's, purchased in 1602), a garden, an orchard and a close, with again numerous elms. Here the Poet could write, without interruption, with his intense concentration and

---

[1] He sold a load of stone to the Chamberlains in 1597–8 apparently after the restoration of his house. [2] I. iii. 41–62.
[3] Notwithstanding what Halliwell-Phillipps has written (in his desire to prove the cause of the Poet's death) of the 'insalubrious state of the Lane'. His evidence goes to show the activity of the authorities in Shakespeare's time in keeping the stream clean, and their characteristic inactivity in the eighteenth century. See further p. 51 f.

phenomenal swiftness, *The Merchant of Venice* and a score
of plays after—among his flowers and fruit-trees, amid the
cooing of pigeons, the beat of the flail, the clack of the water-
mill in the lane,

As fast as mill-wheels strike.[1]

At New Place his daughters grew to womanhood, and
marriage—Susanna with Doctor Hall in 1607, Judith with
Thomas Quyney in 1616. Thomas Greene, his cousin, the
Town Clerk, lived with them and Mistress Shakespeare, a
man in the house (when not keeping his terms in London or on
circuit), probably from 1603 until 1611, with his wife Letitia,
and his children, named significantly *Anne* (in 1604) and
William (in 1608).

15. THE CHAPEL

IN the Chapel the Poet was on familiar ground. Under
his father's auspices as Chamberlain it had been terribly
protestantized. 'Images' were 'defaced' and crosses hacked,
the rood-loft was taken down, and a partition was erected
between the nave and chancel.[2] A communion 'board' replaced the altar.[3] The almsfolk and schoolboys attended
prayers here on week-days conducted by the schoolmaster.
Sermons on special occasions were delivered before the Corporation and leading townsmen. The bailiff and his 'brethren'
were jealous of their right to the Chapel and the order of their
sitting. Sometimes distinguished visitors occupied the pulpit (which was probably in front of the 'partition'). The
champion of English presbyterianism, Thomas Cartwright,
master of Leicester's Hospital in Warwick and protegé of the
Earls of Leicester and Warwick, preached here in 1586 and

---

[1] *The Tempest*, I. ii. 281.
[2] It was removed, and the position of the pulpit changed, in 1641.
[3] *Minutes and Accounts*, I. li. 128, 138 f.

again in 1587.¹ On the former visit he was accompanied by his neighbour and fellow nonconformist, Job Throgmorton of Haseley, just elected Member of Parliament for Warwick (where Shakespeare's kinsmen, the Greenes, were his supporters),² and notorious two or three years later as the 'Martinist', Whitgift's humorous but slashing satirist. The powerful influence of Warwick Castle alone saved Throgmorton, as it saved Cartwright, from his enemy.

Shakespeare knew well the bells in the Tower—the little bell, which called him to school and his father to Council-meetings, and the great bell, which was tolled at sunrise and sunset, on the outbreak of fire, on the passing of the dying, and burial of the dead. The latter tolls in Shakespeare's verse—in Sonnet 71:

> the surly sullen bell
> Give(s) warning to the world that I am fled
> From this vile world with vilest worms to dwell;

in *Venus and Adonis* 701 f.:

> his grief may be compared well
> To one sore sick that hears the passing-bell;

and *Lucrece* 1493–5:

> sorrow, like a heavy-hanging bell,
> Once set on ringing, with his own weight goes;
> Then little strength rings out the doleful knell.

Young Shakespeare had been up the Tower and swung this bell. It was recast in 1591, repaired in 1615 (a few months before Shakespeare's 'passing' and funeral), and again recast in 1633.³

On the bells were struck the hours and quarters of the Clock,

¹ 'Paid to Master Waterman'—at the *Swan*—'for wine given to Master Job Throkmorton and Master Cartwright 3s., for sugar 9d.' (*ib.* iv. 10). 'For wine and sugar bestowed upon Master Cartwright 2s.' (*ib.* 24).
² *Black Book of Warwick*, T. Kemp, pp. 385–97.
³ It is encircled by the initials of the members of the Corporation of that year—including Daniel Baker, Henry Walker, Richard Hathaway, and Thomas Quyney

GREAT BELL IN THE CHAPEL TOWER

(recast 1633)

THE GILD HALL *(from the stage end)*

the dial of which, with a single hand, faced New Place (set at the side of the lower belfry-window, on the west, not, as now, beneath it). A quaint weathercock surmounted the Tower. Below, at the west door, was a little shop, the tenant of which was forbidden to make a fire.

16. THE GILD HALL, SCHOOL, AND COURT

A PASSAGE between the Chapel and the Gild Hall, beneath the assistant-schoolmaster's chamber, led by the door of the Hall (on the right) to the Chapel quad. Within the Hall, among fading or lime-washed frescoes of the old Catholic days (and the account, scribbled on the durable-plaster before it was dry, of an ancient Gild repast), the Poet's father sat and adjudicated as a principal magistrate in the Court of Record. At the south-east corner was the 'Council Chamber' or 'House', where as Bailiff he presided, on his stool, with his hour-glass, at the meetings of his some two-dozen fellow aldermen and burgesses. This chamber made an admirable tiring-house for the players, who erected their stage at the upper end of the Hall. Over the Hall was the Schoolroom, which had been fashioned under John Shakespeare's auspices as Chamberlain out of the old Gild 'dorter'. Above the Council Chamber was the handsome Treasure Chamber (or 'Counting House' of the Gild), containing the 'Great Chest' for Corporation deeds and moneys, iron-bound, with three clasp locks.[1] This chamber was also the Armoury,[2] sometime let to a master-mason and wood-carver, Robert Cox, for his 'workshop'.[3] It held the 'town-harness', or armour and weapons for the trained soldiers. Within the 'Court' or quad were (a) the old Priests' House, (b) the foretime Schoolhouse, and (c) the chamber (*Camera juxta*

[1] In 1614 (Chamberlain's Account 7 Jan. 1613 4). Previously (1585) it stood in the *Camera juxta Aulam* (see n. 3).
[2] In 1614 and previous to Master Cox's occupation in 1585. Whence Petruchio obtained his sword—'an old rusty sword ta'en out of the Town-Armoury' (*Taming of the Shrew*, III. ii. 46).
[3] *Minutes and Accounts*, iii. 164, 171.

Aulam) for the priest-schoolmaster; which underwent various changes until 1590, when Alexander Aspinall obtained possession, and proceeded to convert the second into a dwelling for himself and a wife, the third into quarters for the old curate Gilbert, and the first into a commodious residence for Master Henry Smith, husband of his step-daughter, Anne Shaw, yet another able son of Shakespeare's godfather.[1]

For at least seven years, from 1571 to 1578, Shakespeare learnt Latin—Latin, and again Latin—and happily loved it, Latin prose, Latin verse, and Latin plays, and probably, according to custom in a *Schola Grammaticalis,* performed in these plays, under masters who were Oxford graduates—Walter Roche of Corpus, Simon Hunt, and Thomas Jenkins of St. John's.[2] Hunt is an outstanding figure. His superiority to Roche and Jenkins, in scholarship and character and probably social status, and his influence on Shakespeare, religious as well as academic, may account for the Poet's Latinity and slight regard for schoolmasters generally (though this has been exaggerated), and his undoubted sympathies (at least in his earlier work) with the Old Faith. Hunt, who was licensed to teach in Stratford School by the Bishop of Worcester in October 1571,[3] two and a half years after taking his B.A. at Oxford,[4] did not find Stratford puritanism to his taste, had his windows broken, apparently, in a barring-out, in 1573,[5] turned Roman Catholic, entered Douay University in 1575, was admitted to the Society of Jesus in 1578, succeeded

[1] pp. 15, 32 f.
[2] There is no need (with Arthur Gray, *A Chapter in the Early Life of Shakespeare*) to take the Poet to Polesworth. Stratford was twenty times a better centre of culture and education—and for the upbringing of a page (which Shakespeare never was), as at Arrow, Coughton, Beauchamp Court, Wootton Wawen, Grove Park, Warwick Priory, Warwick Castle, Charlecote, Clopton, Compton Winyates, and a score of aristocratic houses in the neighbourhood.
[3] J. W. Gray, *Shakespeare's Marriage*, p. 108.
[4] *Register of the University of Oxford*, i. 269.
[5] *Minutes and Accounts*, II. xl. 75.

THE COUNCIL CHAMBER

Here John Shakespeare as Bailiff presided at the 'halls' or meetings of the Corporation in 1568–9. This chamber served as a tiring-house for players who performed in the adjoining hall

CHAMBER OVER THE COUNCIL CHAMBER

Father Parsons as English Penitentiary at St. Peter's in 1580, and died at Rome, not much over thirty years of age, in 1585.[1] Presumably he was an accomplished Latinist. Curiously, so interrelated were the clashing creeds, he seems to have been connected with the Harvards.[2] He entrusted £60 to the keeping of William Harvard, brother-in-law of Bishop Watson, and Alderman William Smith of Stratford.

Jenkins did not shine after such a predecessor. Welsh parentage and pronunciation may have rendered him the subject of Shakespeare's wit in the person of 'Sir Hugh Evans'. The lesson to William Page might have been given in Stratford. It is directly from Lily's *A Short Introduction of Grammar* 'generally to be used, compiled and set forth for the bringing up of all those that intend to attain the knowledge of the Latin tongue', of which there were editions in 1567 and 1568. We read there, 'In nouns be two numbers, the singular and the plural. The singular number speaketh of one, as *lapis* a stone.' 'Articles are borrowed of the pronoun and be thus declined: Singulariter, Nominativo *hic haec hoc*, Genitivo *huius*, Dativo *huic*, Accusativo *hunc hanc hoc*, Vocativo caret, Ablativo *hoc hac hoc*. Pluraliter, Nominativo *hi hae haec*, Genitivo *horum harum horum*, Dativo *his*, Accusativo *hos has haec*, Vocativo caret, Ablativo *his*.' Hence the dialogue:

Evans. William, how many numbers is in nouns? *William.* Two. *Evans.* What is *lapis*, William? *William.* A stone. *Evans.* And what is a stone, William? *William.* A pebble. *Evans.* No, it is *lapis*. . . . What is he, William, that does lend articles? *William.* Articles are borrowed of the pronoun, and be thus declined: Singulariter, Nominativo *hic haec hoc*. *Evans.* Nominativo *hig, hag, hog*, pray you, mark. Genitivo *huius*. Well, what is your accusative case? *William.* Accusativo *hinc*. *Evans.* I pray you, have your remembrance, child; accusativo *hung*

---

[1] J. H. Pollen, S.J., *The Month*, Oct.–Nov. 1917.
[2] J. W. Gray, p. 108 f.

hang hog. . . . What is the focative case, William? *William.* O, vocativo *ho. Evans.* Remember, William, focative is *caret.*' [1]

A worthy, stout-hearted, if lowly born and verbose Tudor dominy may have been Jenkins, that made 'fritters of English' notwithstanding his terms at Oxford, and provided features for Fluellen as well as Evans. He was energetic in the musters of 1579, and was paid £6 to resign his mastership in favour of John Cottom. He probably was made a chaplain in the Queen's forces. Cottom may have been a friend of his at Oxford, where he graduated the same year. He came to Stratford from London, and stayed until the autumn of 1582. Then succeeded Alexander Aspinall, M.A., who stayed over forty years.

This gentleman came, by way of Brasenose, from Lancashire with not a little of his countrymen's alleged conceit, that, 'what Lancashire thinks to-day England will think to-morrow'. He was ready to instruct Stratford young or old, an exemplary, dominating person, not only as Schoolmaster for more than a generation, but from time to time as Chamberlain, an Alderman, Deputy Town Clerk, and, on occasion, bum-bailiff, as well as a good man of business in the 'buying and selling of wool and yarn, and making of malt', and the acquisition and letting of Corporation leaseholds. He was facetiously known as 'Great Philip Macedon'. On his betrothal, aged about 42, in 1594 to Widow Shaw of Henley Street,[2] he presented her with the customary pair of ornamented and perfumed gloves,[3] purchased, we may presume, at Alderman Shakespeare's shop, on which the Poet, being at home, wrote the posy—

> The Gift is small, the Will is all:
> Alexander Aspinall.[4]

I am afraid his pupils sometimes stressed the first syllable of his name (it is sometimes spelled Asspinal), as the courtiers in

[1] *The Merry Wives of Windsor*, IV. i. See *Minutes and Accounts*, II. xl f.
[2] p. 18.   [3] *Master Richard Quyny*, p. 62 f.
[4] Commonplace Book of Sir Francis Fane, Fulbeck, 5 May 1672.

'CHAPEL' (*The name given to the precinct*)

Sir Gilbert's Camera
(behind the wall)

Master Aspinall's dwelling
(former School House built
in 1428)

House on site of the
old Priests' House
(the vicarage)

THE OLD CHAMBER FOR THE SCHOOLMASTER (*Camera juxta Aulam*)

Love's Labour's Lost threw after Holofernes the last syllable of his assumed 'Judas'.[1] We need not look farther for the prototype of Holofernes, 'the schoolmaster, exceeding fantastical, too too vain'.[2]

But if Aspinall was 'Holofernes', who was 'Sir Nathaniel' but the guileless curate and clock-setter, Sir William Gilbert *alias* Higgës? This mild and obliging 'minister' lived for years in the Gild precinct, in the *Camera juxta Aulam*, within a dozen yards of 'the pedagogue's house', as Aspinall's dwelling was long denominated. Shakespeare's curate is 'a foolish mild man; an honest man, look you, and soon dashed; a marvellous good neighbour, faith, *and a very good bowler*; but for Alisander, alas, a little o'erparted.'[3] Master Aspinall and Sir Gilbert doubtless played bowls in the Gild Garden.

17. CHURCH STREET

OPPOSITE the Almshouse in Church Street was John Sadler's freehold;[4] a dwelling-house and tenements to the north of it, and premises extending to Dale's Close and Tinkers' Lane—stables, outbuildings, garden, orchard, and dovecote.[5] He was a leading townsman in Shakespeare's youth; and his son, John (born in 1561), and daughter, Margaret (who married William Parsons),[6] and nephew, Hamlet,[7] were among the Poet's earliest friends. He was a miller, tenant of the 'Town Mills' below the Church. He was also tenant or owner of 'walk-mills', including that in Chapel Lane, tenant of several barns, owner of Dovehouse Close in Windsor,[8] owner of the *Bear Inn* in Bridge Street, possessor of timber in his 'forestry' in Church Street, and of ashes and withes at Arlescote.

---

[1] v. ii. 628–31.   [2] v. ii. 531 f.
[3] v. ii. 584–8. Alderman Parsons speaks of him as 'Sir Willy'.
[4] Nos. 11–15: of which 12–15 have just been pulled down (their site, as I write, stands naked to the sky). Is it not time that every ancient house in Stratford was regarded as a National Monument?
[5] See his Will and Inventory (at Worcester '1584 no. 21').
[6] See p. 32.   [7] See p. 33.   [8] Henley or Hell Lane.

As an example of the vigilance of the Corporation, in the proximity of New Place as throughout the town, may be cited their fining of 'John Sadler 16^d for winnowing his peas in Dead Lane,[1] leaving the chaff in the Lane, bringing his swine into the same, and not scouring the ditch there'—4d. for each several offence.[2] This was in 1561, two or three years before his election to the Chamber. His promotion to the aldermanic bench was in John Shakespeare's bailiwick, on the memorable day of Master Perrott's 'fining', 7 September 1569.[3] He served as Bailiff in 1570–1, and would have served again in 1582–3 had his health permitted. The only occasion on which Alderman Shakespeare emerged from his ten years malcontent retirement was to vote for his old friend for this honourable office, on Wednesday 5 September 1582.[4] Sadler died six months later, and was buried in the Church on 12 March 1583.

His will and inventory [5] give a pleasant picture of his comfortable home in Church Street, with his wife, two sons, and three daughters.[6] Shakespeare must have seen him in his 'parlour'—a chamber wainscoted and hung about with 'painted cloths', and furnished with a table that could be 'turned up' after supper like Capulet's,[7] 'a little square table', a chair and three forms with cushions, a crossbow on the wall, a cupboard full of silver, three 'coffers' or chests, and a sumptuous Elizabethan bedstead—a four-poster with curtains, piled up with mattress, flock bed and feather bed, bolsters, pillows, blankets, sheets, and 'hillings' (as coverlets were called), worth £70 at least in our money. His linen was valued at £20— say £200 and more now; his silver, including a fine goblet,[8]

---

[1] Chapel Lane.   [2] *Minutes and Accounts*, i. 117.   [3] *Ib.* ii. 28–30.
[4] *Ib.* iii. 99–101.   [5] Unearthed by Mr. Savage at Worcester.
[6] Margaret the fourth and oldest was married and living in Wood Street.
[7] *Romeo and Juliet*, I. v. 29.
[8] The proverbial miller's pride?—
          In yonder chair I see him sit
          Three fingers round the old silver cup.
                    (Tennyson's *Miller's Daughter*).

THE OVER HALL OF THE GILD (*converted into a Schoolroom*)

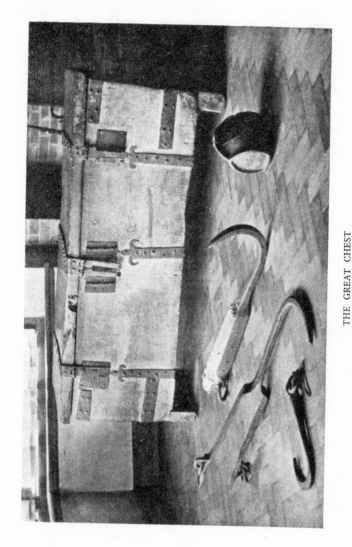

THE GREAT CHEST

With Fire-Hooks (one contains a portion of its pole) and a Leather Bottle such as that referred to in 3 Henry VI. ii. v. 48

at even a higher figure. This goblet he bequeathed to John, his gold signet-ring to his second son, Thomas.

Thomas, who inherited the *Bear*, proved a scapegrace, disposed of the Inn [1] and went to the wars in Ireland, leaving his children to the care of his brother, John, and his wife to the Almshouse. John inherited the Mill, and the rent of the fullers' mill, and the freehold in Church Street on his mother's death. He married Isabella Smart, daughter of Peter Smart of Henley Street, in 1584, just a year before his mother married Alderman Dixon of the *Swan*.[2] Prior to his mother's death in 1609 he lived for some time in Rother Market, next door to John Gibbs. On 10 June 1595 Gibbs was almost killed by a fall of timber—whilst felling, probably, one of the many trees which grew about his house: sixteen elms in his grounds and six more before his door. Sadler sent for a surgeon, Robert Reade. We hear of other medical men in Stratford—Master Hancbeam, surgeon, who died in 1575; Master Philip More, physician, whose wife, a Catholic recusant, found refuge in 1592 at Evesham; and Masters Agge (or Agard), George and John, who practised in and around the parish in the reign of King James. The reputation of all these was eclipsed by that of Shakespeare's son-in-law, the fashionable puritan physician, Doctor John Hall.

Sadler, like his father, served in the Corporation, but less wealthy found it a strain on his resources. He was Bailiff in 1599–1600, and Head Alderman to Richard Quyney, in the latter's second and fatal term of service, in 1601–2. When the time came for Sadler's second bailiwick, 1611, he pleaded his 'decayed estate'. His colleagues, not convinced, elected him in 1612; but in February 1614 they allowed him to retire from the Chamber. If Sadler, however, lacked wealth, he did not

---

[1] He sold it to Anthony Nash, who bequeathed it in 1622 to his son Thomas Nash, the future husband of Shakespeare's granddaughter, Elizabeth Hall, p. 9 note.   [2] p. 3.

want for able children. His son, John Sadler the third, born in 1587, prospered as a grocer and citizen of London; and his daughters, Margaret, Frances, and Eleanor, married men of good family—Leonard Kempson, Peter Baker, Richard Quyney. The last, son of Master Richard Quyney, Shakespeare's friend, was partner in London with his brother-in-law, John Sadler the third. They together presented a silver mace to the Stratford Corporation in 1632. Leonard Kempson, son of Edward Kempson gentleman of Arden's Grafton, lived with his wife in her father's and grandfather's old home. He was a musician, if we may judge from his instruments. Delicate apparently, though he served as constable of his ward in 1601–2, he was a patient of Doctor Hall and died young in August 1625, less than two months after his father-in-law. Among his effects were 'a pair of virginals', two viols, a cittern, a recorder, a flute, and 'music-books'. These treasures add beauty to the house of the Sadlers, of which we have a further glimpse in John the second's will and inventory. He lay dying in his father's bed, in the handsome parlour of forty-two years since, and declared:

'I, John Sadler, gentleman, sick in body but in good and perfect memory . . . bequeath my soul into the hands of Almighty God . . . and my body . . . to be buried in the church of Stratford. . . . I give to my son, John Sadler, of London, *the bed and whole furniture thereunto belonging, in the parlour where I lie*, . . . *one frame and joined table . . . forms, all the wainscot and painted cloths . . . cushions . . . chairs . . . great cupboard*', and so forth.[1]

Little is changed since his father's death, save that the silver is gone, and the crossbow, and in the inner chamber is a 'great leather chest' full of pewter, and a fine copy of the English Bible valued at 13s. 4d.[2] Music and the Bible are significant marks of contemporary culture.

In Tinkers' Lane, to which the Sadler premises extended,

[1] Misc. Doc. vi. 65.   [2] *Ib.* i. 21.

was the Pinfold or Pound erected on land belonging to the Almshouse in John Shakespeare's energetic chamberlainship.[1] It may be responsible for the Poet's youthful witticism in *The Two Gentlemen of Verona*:

> *Proteus.* Nay, in that you are astray, 'twere best pound you.
> *Speed.* Nay, sir, less than a pound shall serve me for carrying your letter.
> *Proteus.* You mistake; I mean the Pound, a pinfold.
> *Speed.* From a pound to a pin? fold it over and over,
>   'Tis threefold too little for carrying to your lover.[2]

Lower down Church Street, on the left, was the house, with adjoining tenements, of Robert Salisbury the brewer, who succeeded John Shakespeare as bailiff in the anxious time of the Northern Rebellion, 1569, when the Queen of Scots was in the neighbourhood. He may have followed Robert Perrott the brewer in these premises, who had property next door, including a dwelling-house long leased to the Corporation for the Vicar. Perrott let this house in 1550 to the late subwarden of the College, Edward Alcock, LL.B. of Cambridge, for a term of thirty-one years at the rent of 24s. The Corporation acquired the lease, and here lived the first Protestant incumbents—John Bretchgirdle, M.A. (who baptized Shakespeare), 1561–5; William Smart, B.A., 1565–7; William Butcher, M.A., B.D., late President of Corpus Christi College, Oxford, who 'being *in animo Catholicus*', was deprived at the time of the Northern Rebellion; Henry Haycroft, M.A., of Cambridge (who baptized Shakespeare's daughter Susanna), 1569–84; Richard Barton, a puritan preacher from Coventry (who baptized Shakespeare's twins, Judith and Hamnet), 1584–9; John Rushton, B.A., of (? St. John's) Oxford; John Bramhall, M.A., of Oxford, 1589–96 (who attributed the fires of 1594 and 1595 to breaking of the Sabbath); Richard Byfield, 'Professor of Sacred Theology' (father of two sons who went to

---

[1] *Min. and Acc.* i. 128 and notes.   [2] I. i. 110–16.

Oxford and became noted puritan preachers), 1596–1605; and John Rogers, M.A., of Oxford (who buried Shakespeare), a follower of Cartwright, at Bifield (1589)[1] and St. Nicholas, Warwick (1599–1605), before his ministry in Stratford, 1605–19. On the expiration of the Alcock lease in 1581, the house was let by Perrott's son-in-law and representative, and subsequent heir, Richard Woodward, at the enhanced rent of 40s. In 1605 the Corporation sought another residence as vicarage, decided provisionally on John Tomlins's house (next door but two to New Place), then on a house in Church Street (next door to the Sadlers'); but in 1606 they removed the discontented Rogers to Master Gibbs's house in Rother Street. Eventually, on the expiration of Aspinall's lease of the old Priests' House in the Chapel Quad, they determined on this for the vicar, and in 1611 Rogers and his family were settled here in place of the Henry Smiths.[2] The change for Aspinall must have been disturbing. The vicar had four children, by August 1612, wanted a stable for his horse, and a wood-house, and a pigsty. The Corporation were prepared to erect a stable and a wood-house against the mud-wall of the Schoolmaster's garden, but would not allow the pigsty (to which Shakespeare may have objected) on the Lane side. This was in 1613.[3] Rogers, moreover, had 'faults and failings', which the Corpora-

[1] 'Go to, Brother Thomas [Cartwright], tell your neighbours about you—Rogers of Bifield, Fenn of Coventry, and the rest—that I keep a register of all the puritan purchasers in the realm' (Nash, *The Return of Pasquil*, McKerrow, i. 99).   [2] p. 48.
[3] Rogers pleaded for his pigsty, that he might 'finish that small pleck' (patch of ground) 'which I have begun in the Lane, the use whereof was no other but to keep a swine or two in ; for about my house there is no place of convenience without much annoyance to the Chapel; and how far the breeding of such creatures is needful to poor house-keepers I refer myself to those who can equal my charge.' But the Borough fathers were obdurate—as they had been with the previous tenant, Henry Smith, whom they bade on 22 August 1605 'to pluck down his pigscote near the Chapel Wall and the house of office there, and forbear to keep any swine about the house or Chapel Yard' (Council Book B, p. 126).

tion hoped he would 'amend' on their gift to him of a new gown. He did not improve; and they obtained his resignation on his inadvertent acceptance of another benefice in 1619. He had friends, who made an unseemly riot in his favour in the Church on Sunday 30 May; but before Christmas the vicarage was under repair for his successor, a brilliant young preacher from Evesham, Thomas Wilson, B.D., of Oxford, not improbably grandson of the late Dean of Worcester.

18. OLD TOWN

NEAR the entrance to Old Town, on our right, were the house and garden, with a barn (and a public refuse-heap before it), in the tenure successively of Richard Smith dyester (or dyer), his son William Smith haberdasher (of Henley Street), and his grandson, *Master* John Smith vintner (of High Street): worthy of our notice because of the association of these Smiths with the Shakespeares. Below, on the boundary between the New and Old Town, was the Tithe Barn within and without the mud-wall of the College grounds. The College faced the Church, and its grounds were parted from the churchyard by Mill Lane. Between Mill Lane and Evesham Lane was Lime Close, commonly known as 'Lord's Close'; and more correctly, for the limes were all gone, and 67 elms, 9 ashes, and 2 crab-trees grew in their place. On our left were 'Hall's Croft', the Clopton Dower-House, and in the 'Church Way' the house of the Reynolds, then St. Mary's House adjoining the graveyard.

There is nothing in local records to confirm or discredit the tradition that 'Hall's Croft' was the home of Doctor Hall before his residence at New Place. We know little of him prior to his marriage. He was, doubtless, the John Hall who matriculated at Oxford from Balliol on 4 February 1592, aged sixteen, the son of a Worcestershire 'gentleman'—a kinsman perhaps of Master Richard Hall of Idlicote, who had associations with

Stratford, and was overseer of the will of George Whateley of Henley Street in 1593. He took his B.A. in 1595 and M.A. (from St. Edmund's Hall) in 1598.[1] From Oxford he went to a Continental University, as many medical students did, and obtained a degree probably in France.[2] He was seven years older than his wife, Susanna Shakespeare, and only twelve years younger than her father, who shows an entirely new interest in medical matters in his plays after friendship with him—in *Hamlet, Macbeth, King Lear,* and the dramas that followed. In Stratford the Doctor enjoyed a large and fashionable practice, extending into and beyond the neighbouring shires. Catholics were among his patients, notwithstanding his puritan principles—wherein he seems to have had the full sympathy of his wife.[3] He was a warm admirer and friend, and champion, of the vicar, Thomas Wilson. In 1626 he declined a knighthood on the coronation of King Charles, paying a £10 fine for his refusal.

The foundations of St. Mary's House are still to be seen. Hither Thomas Greene removed with his family from New Place in 1611, and here was born in 1612 his daughter, Elizabeth—of the same name as Shakespeare's granddaughter, the only child of the Halls. He had bought the house, and he spent freely on it, converting it, as he said, into a 'pretty, neat, gentlemanlike' residence, 'in a little young orchard'.[4] Eldest son of Master Thomas Greene, mercer, in the High Pavement, Warwick, educated at Staple Inn and the Middle Temple, a bencher, and before long Reader and Treasurer of the Middle Temple, Town Clerk and Steward of Stratford, he was probably, next to the Poet and Doctor Hall, the ablest man in the

---

[1] *Register,* II. ii. 187, iii. 190. 'Jo. Hall, *generosus, in Artibus Magister*' is the entry of his name on the list of Burgesses, 30 June 1632.
[2] 'He had been a traveller acquainted with the French tongue' (*Select Observations,* 1657). John Bird, Linacre Professor at Oxford, spoke of 'the learned author' and the 'great fame' of 'his skill far and near' (*ib.*).
[3] See p. 77 f.
[4] Misc. Doc. vii. 125.

town. Like Doctor Hall, he was something of a poet. Hall,
we may believe, wrote the Latin verses on his mother-in-law's
tomb as a panegyric from his wife:

> *Ubera, tu mater, tu lac vitamque dedisti;*
> *Vae mihi, pro tanto munere saxa dabo?*
> *Quam mallem amoveat lapidem bonus angelus ore!*
> *Exeat, ut Christi corpus, imago tua!*
> *Sed nil vota valent; venias cito, Christe! resurget,*
> *Clausa licet tumulo, mater et astra petet.*[1]

The 'angelus' is that of Matthew xxviii. 2, Mark xvi. 3, of
which he had read in the Vulgate—*angelus revolvit lapidem . . .
ab ostio monumenti*. The examples of Greene's poetry are
little known—a sonnet complimenting Michael Drayton in the
latter's collected *Poems* of 1605,[2] and Latin verses in his diary
on 'Death'. The sonnet, more in the strain of Drayton[3] than
of Shakespeare, runs:

> What ornament might I devise to fit
> Th'aspiring height of thy admired spirit?
> Or what fair garland worthy is to sit
> On thy blest brows, that compass in all merit?
> Thou shalt not crownèd be with common bays,
> Because for thee it is a crown too low;
> Apollo's tree can yield thee simple praise—
> It is too dull a vesture for thy brow;
> But with a wreath of stars shalt thou be crown'd,
> Which, when thy working temples do sustain,
> Will like the spheres be ever moving round
> After the royal music of thy brain:

[1] 'Breasts, Mother, milk and life thou gavest me; alack, for so great a
boon shall I give stones? How much rather I wish the good angel
to remove the stone from the mouth, thine image to come forth as did
the body of Christ! But prayers avail nothing—Come quickly,
Christ! though shut in the tomb may my mother rise again and seek
the stars.'

[2] There seems no reason to ascribe this poem to Thomas Greene the
actor.

[3] Cf. Drayton's lines on Marlowe, and *A Mid. N. Dream*, v. i. 4–17.

Thy skill doth equal Phoebus, not thy birth;
He to Heaven gives music, thou to earth.

The Latin, which contains phrases in general use and a couplet found elsewhere,[1] is the expression of private anxiety and piety at Christmas time 1614:[2]

> *Heu! vivunt homines tanquam mors nulla sequetur,*
>   *Et velut informis fabula vana fide.*
> *Mors certa est, incerta dies, hora agnita nulli;*
>   *Extremam quare quamlibet esse puta.*
> *Fleres si scires unum tibi tempora mensem,*
>   *Rides cum non sit forsitan una dies.*
> *Qui modo sanus erat nunc lecto egrotus adheret,*
>   *Estque cinis subito qui modo civis erat.*[3]

On Shakespeare's death Greene resigned his clerkship, sold his house, and went to live in Bristol. In a letter of May 1617 to his old friends in the Stratford Corporation, whom he had led with singular ability in defence of their rights against the younger Combes, he spoke of his 'golden days' in their service.[4] We cannot doubt that it was the Poet's friendship and kinship which made these days of strenuous labour 'golden', and his death which turned sunshine into night. Greene died in Bristol, or at his chambers in London, in 1640.[5]

---

[1] *Mors certa est* is Englished by Shallow, 2 *Henry IV*, III. ii. 40 f. The religious preamble of Perrott's will begins, 'Seeing all men are mortal and nothing more certain than death, although nothing more uncertain than the hour thereof' (8 March 1589). The lines *Fleres* . . . *Rides* occur in St. Sebald's, Nuremberg.

[2] 21 December, a few days before his wife's confinement, whose child was baptized on the 30th—Thomas.

[3] 'Alack! men live as though no death will follow, and as if it were a hideous fable devoid of credit. Death is certain, uncertain the day, the hour known to none; think therefore any day to be thy last. Thou would'st weep if thou knewest thy time to be but a month; thou dost laugh when perchance it may be but a day. He who late was in health now keeps his bed sick, and he of late a citizen is straightway a cinder.'

[4] Misc. Doc. i. 1.   [5] See his Will, P. C. C. 88 Evelyn.

19. THE COLLEGE

'THE College', or ancient priests' house (*Domum Collegii*) of the college dissolved in 1535, was a handsome edifice of hewn stone in extensive grounds, leased to the Barkers, and under them held by the Combes. By husbandry and law, the acquisition of monastic property, leases and ownership of land, and money-lending, the Combes grew rich until they almost rivalled the Cloptons and Lucys. John Combe of Astley married in 1534, for his second wife, Katharine Quyney, the widow of Adrian Quyney's grandfather,[1] and settled in Stratford, where he was welcomed as a friend of the New Learning, and became a colleague on commissions with Master William Lucy, the father of Sir Thomas. He died in 1550, a few months before William Lucy, leaving a son by a first wife, John. This son, John Combe the second of Stratford, dropped, if he ever held, the heretical opinions, lived through the reign of Mary, and was reported in 1564 'an adversary of the True Religion'; by which the reporter, the ultra-Protestant William Hudson of Warwick, meant sound puritan doctrine. He died about 1567, leaving two sons, who interest us, William Combe the lawyer and John Combe of Stratford the third.

William entered the Middle Temple in 1571, settled in Warwick, where he was greatly respected ('an honest gentleman, their neighbour, well-known to them all')[2] and in 1592 elected Member of Parliament; while retaining a close connexion with Stratford, for which he was counsel from 1597 to his death. Shakespeare bought land of him in 1602. On the decease of his wife, Alice, in 1606 he married Lady Jane, widow of Sir William Puckering, Keeper of the Great Seal. He died in 1610,[3] leaving no children but a large estate, the

---

[1] Hence the kinship of the Quyneys and Shakespeares (after 10 Feb. 1616) with the Combes.
[2] *Black Book of Warwick*, p. 405.
[3] He was buried in St. Nicholas, Warwick.

bulk of which he bequeathed to his brother's son and grandson
in Stratford. He was a grave man, like his junior bencher,
Thomas Greene. His will,[1] drawn up on Sunday 1 April 1610,
opens with religious reflection and prayer:

Omnis gloria Dei et omnis salus hominum in Christi morte con-
    stituta sunt.
Audi, Fili, verba oris mei eaque in corde Tuo quasi fundamentum
    repone!
Nescit homo diem suam: dies nostra quasi umbra super terram et
    nulla mora.[2]

Such utterances, and there are more in this solemn document,
were not formalities.

John Combe the third, elder brother of William, was agent
to the lord of the manor of Stratford (Ambrose Earl of
Warwick), gathered his rents, held leases from him and others,
married four times (twice at least his wife was a lady of means),
and lent money to neighbours at ten and twelve per cent. In
1590 he had, among others, two grown-up sons well known
to Shakespeare, Thomas who married twice and had sons,
William and Thomas; and John, John Combe the fourth, who
remained a bachelor, and lived at Welcombe.

Thomas was apparently an author. On 9 May 1593 was
entered to Richard Field at Stationer's Hall 'a book intituled
*The Theatre of Fine Devices, containing An Hundred Moral
Emblems translated out of French by Thomas Combe*'.[3] Three
weeks previously, on 18 April, Shakespeare's *Venus and Adonis*
had been entered to the same publisher from Stratford. The
conjunction more than suggests literary sympathy between the
Birthplace and the College. Would that we knew more of

[1] P.C.C. 52 Wood.
[2] 'All the glory of God and all the salvation of men are established
in the Death of Christ. Hearken, O Son, to the words of my mouth,
and lay them in Thine heart as my foundation! Man knoweth not his
day: our day is as a shadow upon earth nor is there any delay.'
[3] Arber, ii. 631.

Thomas Combe and his Hundred Moral Emblems from the French! We read in the Corn Inquiry of 1595 that he had seventeen quarters of wheat and rye and fifty-two of barley (presumably stored in the old Tithe Barn, in his half of it, the other half being Corporation property), had seven quarters of malt, and 'was of household fourteen persons', but no copy of his book has come to light. In 1596 he purchased the College—a few months before Shakespeare's purchase of New Place. They thus owned the two chief residences of Stratford, one in the 'Old' Town, the other in the 'New'. Thomas Combe died in 1609 leaving the College to his elder son, William.

John Combe the bachelor is more associated with usury than with literature; but like his uncle, William the lawyer of Warwick, he was a grave man, was honoured for his 'virtue' (probably his integrity in keeping a contract), and was the founder of a preachership. The religious opening of his will[1] (drawn up by Francis Collins) closely resembles that of Shakespeare's will (drawn up by the same lawyer). He signed it on 28 January 1613, eighteen months nearly before his death; whence we may conclude that his thankfulness for 'perfect health and memory' was not a legal fiction, and that the Poet, in praising God for the same in January 1616, did not anticipate immediate dissolution. His bequests include, 'to Master William Shakespeare £5, to Master Henry Walker 20s., unto Sir Francis Smith' of Wootton Wawen '£5 to buy him a hawk, and to the Lady Anne his wife £40 to buy her a basin and ewer'. He left £20 to a god-daughter, £10 to a godson, and 5s. to 'every one' of his 'god-children not named'. 'A learned preacher' was to receive 20s. for 'a sermon twice a year at Stratford Church'.

If Combe had any qualms of conscience for his usury, his justification would probably have been his benevolence. His charities were considerable—to poor folk 'ten black gowns,

[1] P.C.C. 118 Rudd.

every one worth 13s. 4d.' (wherein to follow him to the grave),
'to the poor of Stratford £20', 'to 15 poor or young tradesmen'
£100 on loan, '20 nobles apiece for 3 years, paying 3s. 4d.
interest at Michaelmas and Lady Day'. He left £100 also to
three old servants.

Usury, and its parents, 'the enhancing of rents' and enclosure of common land, had been denounced in the old Faith
and by the early Reformers, nor were they approved by
leading Protestant divines in Shakespeare's lifetime.

'Usury', complained Harrison, 'a trade brought in by the Jews,
is practised so commonly that he is accounted a fool that doth
lend his money for nothing. In time past it was *sors pro sorte*,
that is, principal only for the principal; now, beside *usura* we
challenge *foenus*—that is, commodity of soil and fruits of the
earth, if not the ground itself.'[1]

Combe in his will 'released' a shilling in the pound to all his
'good and just debtors'; but the bequest did not save his
reputation. On his tomb were 'fastened' (sometime before
1618) the lines:

> Ten-in-the-Hundred must lie in his grave,
> But a hundred to ten, whether God will him have.
> Who then must be interr'd within this tomb?
> 'Oh, oh,' quoth the Devil, 'my John a Combe!'[2]

This doggerel (and Shakespeare wrote masterly doggerel
when it suited his purpose) was ascribed to the Poet before the
year 1634. Shakespeare's Antonio 'lent out money gratis' and
brought down 'the rate of usance' exacted by the Jews in
Venice; and that manly embodiment of unsophisticated

[1] ii. 10.
[2] Aubrey gives an interesting variant, possibly more correct:
> Ten in the hundred the Devil allows;
> But Combe will have twelve, he swears and (a)vows.
> If any one asks who lies in this tomb,
> 'Oh,' quoth the Devil, 'tis my John o' Combe.

nature, the Bastard, rails against 'commodity, the bias of the world':

> The world, who of itself is peised well,
> Made to run even upon even ground,
> Till this advantage, this vile-drawing bias,
> This sway of motion, this Commodity,
> Makes it take head from all indifferency,[1]
> From all direction, purpose, course, intent.[2]

The younger Combes, William and Thomas, nephews of the old 'capitalist', are associated more with landlord monopoly and oppression than with loans on cruel terms to the necessitous. William inherited the College, and lands of his father and of his great-uncle William the lawyer of Warwick; Thomas, lands of his uncle, John the usurer. Their accession of fortune seems to have turned their heads. They proceeded to bully the tenantry, turn the arable land of the commoners into pasture, dig ditches and make mounds for enclosures, defy the Corporation and incite them to 'riot', in the hope thereby to bring the law and king's authority against them. Shakespeare knew these young bloods, and did not take them seriously, until Greene's repeated solicitation and Master Barber's death drew him into the controversy. He supported the Corporation in the last few months of his life.[3] He left nothing to the blustering young *dominus* of the College (now his kinsman); his 'sword' (worn by him as a King's man on state occasions) he

---

[1] Impartiality, justice, fairness.   [2] *King John*, II. i. 575–80.
[3] Whether we read 'I' or 'he' in the entry in Greene's diary in the beginning of September 1615 ('W. Shakespeare's telling J. Greene that I? was not able to bear the enclosing of Welcombe'), it can only mean that Shakespeare had said to the Town Clerk's brother, 'I am not able to bear the enclosing of Welcombe'. There seems no reason why Shakespeare should tell John Greene what John Greene must have known for a twelvemonth, and Shakespeare must have known was known to him, nor why Thomas Greene should record so superfluous a communication. On the other hand, there was ground for relief in the news that Shakespeare had at length definitely expressed himself on the matter. If 'I' is correct, we must read the sentence as *oratio recta*. Greene is rather a stickler for *ipsissima verba*.

bequeathed to the brother—with possibly the ironical reminder that those 'who take the sword shall perish with the sword'.[1] Thomas Combe could take to his fists, and his feet, in his rage beating and kicking a shepherd on Meon.[2]

20. THE CHURCH[3]

BETWEEN the College and St. Mary's House ran the 'Churchway', to the graveyard, and the paths there of which Puck speaks in *A Midsummer Night's Dream*:

> Now it is the time of night
> That the graves, all gaping wide,
> Every one lets forth his sprite,
> In the churchway paths to glide.[4]

The chief one led, probably then as now, under an avenue, to the North porch of the church. The graveyard had many trees in it, and we might hardly see on our left the ancient 'bone-house' on the north side of the chancel. This quaint edifice, consisting of a chamber above and a vault beneath, partly underground, served the twofold purpose of a sleeping-room for the four boys of the old singing-school and a receptacle for skeletons taken from graves to make room for the newly dead. The chamber had become a minister's study in Shakespeare's time, but we are not surprised that the building had gruesome associations in the youthful mind. Juliet refers to it, and to the tower above, in her passionate speech—

> O, bid me leap, rather than marry Paris,
> From off the battlements of yonder tower; . . .

[1] Matthew xxvi. 52. Cf. 2 *Henry VI*, IV. iv. 11.
[2] About Easter (9 April) 1615.
[3] There were two other churches in the wide-spreading parish, at Bishopton and Luddington, where baptisms and marriages, but not burials, could be conducted. They were called Chapels. Shakespeare was familiar with the distinction: e.g. in *As You Like It*, III. iii. 65, 85 : *Touchstone*. Sir Oliver Martext . . . shall we go with you to your chapel? *Jaques*. Get you to church, and have a good priest that can tell you what marriage is—i.e. a preacher, not merely a 'reading minister'.
[4] V. ii. 9–12.

THE SANCTUARY KNOCKER

THE BONE-HOUSE

INTERIOR OF THE BONE-HOUSE

Or shut me nightly in a charnel-house,
O'er-cover'd quite with dead men's rattling bones,
With reeky shanks and yellow chapless skulls.[1]

The girl's horror (she is only fourteen) is that of the Poet's boyhood, something of which was with him to the end. A few feet from the 'bone-house' was his grave within the Chancel (a door connected the Chancel with the 'bone-house'), and as a warning to the sexton[2] he made the epitaph, 'a little before his death',[3] which the rudest clerk could comprehend:

Good Friend, for Jesus' sake forbear
To dig the dust enclosed here:
Blest be the man that spares these stones,
And curst be he that moves my bones.

Burials, we may note, speedily followed death, and sometimes took place at night. The well-to-do were interred in coffins, the poor in their winding-sheets. Ophelia was borne in her shroud in an open coffin (Laertes takes her 'once more' in his 'arms.')[4] In the handsome North Porch, with a chamber over it for the clerk or sexton ('sacristan', not grave-digger) and his registers, was transacted important legal business, such as the payment, and repayment on their day, of loans in the presence of witnesses. Here, too, at the inner door into the Church (*ad ostium ecclesie*), were celebrated marriages, followed by the drinking of healths, distribution of sweetmeats, and occasional unseemly rollicking, so inimitably burlesqued in *The Taming of the Shrew*.[5] On the inner door was (and is) a fine old handle and knocker,[6] which Shakespeare must often have seen and touched. It would serve for that on the abbey gate in *The Comedy of Errors*.[7] At the west end of the Church

[1] *Romeo and Juliet*, IV. i. 77 f., 81–3.
[2] William Hall to Edward Thwaites in 1694 (*Outlines*, ii. 72).
[3] So Dowdall heard from the old sexton, William Castle, in 1693 (*Outlines*, ii. 71 f.). Castle, who was born in 1614, resigned his post as sexton in 1698, and died in 1701.
[4] *Hamlet*, V. i. 273 (both Q and F mention 'coffin').   [5] III. ii. 151–83.
[6] It is known as the ' Sanctuary Knocker'.   [7] V. i. 37, 165.

children were baptized, in the old Gothic font,[1] usually on a Sunday or other holy-day, in the middle of the service,[2] in the presence of a congregation as well as the father (not the mother, who afterwards came for her churching), the godfather, and two godmothers or 'gossips', and family friends. A christening, especially of the child of an alderman (as Shakespeare was), was a public function, followed by a feast at home or at the house of one of the gossips.[3] We must bear in mind, in our study of family relationship, the prominence and significance of sponsorship.[4]

Porch and Nave and Chancel had suffered in the Reformation. As at the Chapel,[5] the 'popish' chancel had been boarded-off from the rest of the Church. After neglect it was made a burial-place for more wealthy inhabitants. The whole Church, indeed, was employed for this purpose. Townsmen liked to be buried at the end of their 'accustomed seat'. Pew rights had become private and were jealously regarded. The New Place pew was on the south side of the nave, near the pulpit. That of the Bailiff and his Brethren, and their wives, was on the north side, adjoining the College pew of the Combes.[6] The Almsfolk had seats at the back. The pulpit was against the middle of the chancel partition, a two—if not three —decker. The service was 'read' [7] by the curate below, the sermon preached by the vicar above. The sexton led the responses and alternate verses of the psalms, a small choir the singing of the canticles and metrical psalms (which were the chief, if not the only, hymns). Congregational singing was

[1] Still in existence, in a broken condition.
[2] 'Baptism should not be ministered but upon Sundays and other holy days, when the most number of people may come together . . . after the last Lesson' (Rubric 1558).
[3] 'A gossips' feast' (*Comedy of Errors*, v. i. 405).
[4] See pp. 15, 36, 40, 45, 63.   [5] p. 45.
[6] Inquiry by Dr. Brent, 5 June 1635, and other papers at the Birthplace.
[7] He was called the 'Reading Minister'.

remarkable at this time for its heartiness. The curate wore, or should have worn, a surplice, the vicar preached in a black gown. Communicants did not kneel and sip the wine from priestly hands, but drank it sitting in their pews, as it was distributed solemnly by the churchwardens, eight or ten quarts of claret at a 'communion', some half a dozen times a year.[1] Wilson was not the only vicar who did things 'amiss'.[2] Liberties were taken with the Prayer Book widely in Elizabeth's reign (especially before the defeat of the Armada, after which fear and hatred of Rome began to subside) and only in a less degree in the reign of James. Shakespeare shows considerable acquaintance with the Prayer Book, but not the intimate knowledge he reveals of the Bible. He heard the Bishops' Bible in church—he was more familiar far with the Geneva Version, which he read at home and probably at school. He evidently joined in the metrical psalms, four of them at least he quotes.[3] He suffered no doubt from a feeble sermon in a cold church:

> When all aloud the wind doth blow,
> And coughing drowns the parson's saw;[4]

but he heard good ones, as we gather from such a passage as,

> And this our life exempt from public haunt,
> Finds tongues in trees, books in the running brooks,
> *Sermons* in stones, and *good* in every thing:
> I would not change it.[5]

---

[1] In 1623 the Chamberlains paid 40s. 4d. for 61 quarts of claret-wine, and 3s. 2d. for bread (from Shakespeare's nephew, Richard Hathaway), for seven 'communions', on Sundays 2 Feb. (Candlemas) 2 March (Lent), 6 July (Midsummer), 3 August (Lammas), 5 October (Michaelmas and Corporation Election and Sermon), 2 November (All Soul's), and 14 December (Christmas).

[2] The irregularities were pronounced in Coventry.

[3] The 24th (2 *Henry VI*, IV. ix. 13 f.), 30th (*Richard II*, V. i. 13 f.), 49th (*Merry Wives*, I. iii. 94 f., II. i. 117 f.), and 137th (*ib.* III. i. 13 ff.)

[4] *Love's Labour's Lost*, V. ii. 931 f.

[5] *As You Like It*, II. i. 15-18. 'Books', too, are 'good'.

The Church-bells (a set of five, brought from Hailes Abbey in 1558) were dear to him:

> If ever been where bells have knoll'd to church [1]—

and the Sacrament was sacred:

> the floor of heaven
> Is thick inlaid with *patines* of bright gold; [2]
> those springs
> On *chaliced* flowers that lies. [3]

His religion slips from him rather than is professed, and is the deeper on this account. Invariably he uses the language of piety of anything he greatly loves—'field-dew *consecrate*', 'this *hallowed* house', '*holy* wedlock', '*bless* with sweet peace', '*holy* innocence', 'drops that *sacred* pity hath engendered', '*Holy* cords too intrinse to unloose', &c., &c. This is better than confessions and creeds.

At the end of the north aisle of the nave he saw, as may we, the Clopton monuments. William Clopton, who died in 1592 a Catholic recusant, and his wife Anne lie in effigy in alabaster. Above are their children, including Joyce, who married Sir George Carew, a cousin of Raleigh, and died a countess. She and her husband in effigy are the finest pieces of sculpture in the Church. In the south transept is a monument of very different artistic merit, the work of some local mason, but of great interest. It is the memorial to Master Richard Hill, [4] the woollen-draper of Wood Street, whose daughter married Abraham Sturley, and step-daughter Daniel Baker, thus linking in kinship these puritan worthies. [5] The graver has made a hash of the Hebrew and Greek in the inscription;

[1] *As You Like It*, II. vii. 114 (and 121, repeated).
[2] *Merchant of Venice*, v. i. 58 f.   [3] *Cymbeline*, II. iii. 23 f.
[4] His initials and those of his fellow churchwarden, Nicholas Tibbotts, are inscribed on a stone over the window with the date '1589', a record of restoration.   [5] p. 32.

JOHN COMBE THE BACHELOR

In effigy on his tomb, carved by Garret Johnson, 1614–15

MONUMENT OF MASTER RICHARD HILL

which pieces of learning, and four Latin rhyming hexameters
we may ascribe to Sturley, as to Baker we may attribute the
English verses concluding:

> He did not use to swear, to glose or feign,
> His brother to defraud in bargaining;
> He would not strive to get excessive gain
> In any cloth or other kind of thing:
> His servant I this truth can testify,
> A witness that beheld it with my eye.

The Hebrew is the text from Job i. 21:

עָרֹם יָצָתִי מִבֶּטֶן אִמִּי, וְעָרֹם אָשׁוּב שָׁמָּה,
יהוה נָתַן ויהוה לָקָח, יְהִי שֵׁם ירוה מְבֹרָךְ

'Naked came I out of my mother's womb and naked shall I
return thither; the Lord hath given, and the Lord hath taken,
blessed be the name of the Lord.'[1]

The two lines of Greek contain a puritan thought and an
expression familiar to Shakespeare as to Sidney:

> Κρύπτει τό ἰλυῶδες δέμας γῆ καὶ ταφή
> ὅτε πνεῦμα καὶ ψυχὴν οὐρανοῦ ὕψος ἔχει.

'The muddy stature earth and tomb conceal, when the
Height of Heaven has mind and spirit.'

Ἰλυῶδες, 'muddy', is probably from Galen. Sturley has
'muddy stature' (δέμας), Shakespeare 'muddy vesture':

> Such harmony is in immortal souls,
> But whilst this muddy vesture of decay
> Doth grossly close it in, we cannot hear it.[2]

In Sidney we read, 'the final end is to lead and draw us to as
high a perfection as our degenerate souls, made worse by their
clayey lodgings, can be capable of'.[3]

---

[1] Geneva Version.   [2] *Merchant of Venice*, v. i. 63–5.
[3] *An Apologie for Poetrie*, 1595 (Arber, p. 29). Cf. 'earthly prisons'
in the 'prayer for a Sick Person' added to the Prayer Book in 1661.

21. THE CHANCEL

THE Chancel, happily, never endured the indignities inflicted upon the chancel of the Chapel by a vicar resident in the adjoining quad. That unfortunate edifice, erected in 1452, too recently to be included in Sir Hugh Clopton's rebuilding of the Chapel in 1496, suffered under John Shakespeare's defacing in 1563,[1] still more from the contemptuous treatment of Thomas Wilson, who used it for his children to play in, his servants to dry clothes in, his pigs to lie in, and his poultry to roost in, to the further destruction of the paintings and glass, until in 1635 the Corporation protested to the Bishop against the profanity.[2] If there had been any real respect for it, or revenue to derive from it, as a place of burial, they would have protested long before.[3] In 1593 the Chancel

Hill's monument was erected after his death in 1593. *The Merchant of Venice* was written, probably at New Place, in 1597.

[1] *Minutes and Accounts*, i. 128, 138 f.   [2] Brent's Visitation.

[3] Wilson's popularity with the Corporation for his preaching in 1619 and until 1626 had turned to personal dislike and antagonism in 1629. The misuse of the Chapel chancel was less objectionable than the man in 1635. That his theology was not at fault is evidenced by the eagerness of the Corporation to obtain the services of Robert Harris of Hanwell as his successor. This leading puritan divine, born at Broad Campden in 1578, matriculated at Oxford from Magdalen Hall in 1595, took his B.A. in 1601 and his B.D. (after being for ten years a student of theology) in 1614. He was preacher at Hanwell after the deprivation of John Dodd, with whom he signed young Daniel Baker's certificate for his M.A. in 1612; and in July 1614 he delivered the funeral sermon for Sir Anthony Cope, whose memorial lines in Latin he composed for his tomb. He became assistant to Rogers at Stratford, and also assistant to Aspinall in the School, just before Shakespeare's death; returned to Hanwell, and had the honour of preaching at Paul's Cross on Sunday 30 June 1622. He was greatly liked in Stratford, and was invited to give a weekly lecture, 'either in the Church or Chapel', in July 1629, the Corporation 'undertaking to satisfy him'. Sir Thomas Lucy the Third came from Charlecote to hear him. He preached for a twelvemonth, and was 'wooed' to come for another year. On Wilson's death in 1638 the Corporation sent a deputation to the Earl of Middlesex to obtain Harris for their vicar, who, however, remained with the Copes at Hanwell. Henry Twitchett,

of the Church was in a bad state, and the Corporation moved
Lord Treasurer Burleigh (the Chancel was Crown property) to
compel the tithe-holders to put it in repair; and not long after
obtaining it as a grant from the Crown, they proceeded to
bring pressure upon these gentlemen, of whom Shakespeare
was one, and to sell, or let, the right of burial within its walls.
Shakespeare was buried here in 1616; but it was not until his
monument was erected, or was about to be erected, that they
had the place made less unworthy of its illustrious dead, and
we may suspect that George Quyney, the reading-minister
from 1620 to 1624, was largely, if not chiefly, responsible for
the reparation. A child two years old when his father, Richard
Quyney, Shakespeare's friend, died in his bailiwick,[1] George
went apparently to Cambridge and thence to Oxford, where he
took his B.A. from Balliol in 1621.[2] For two years he was
assistant to Aspinall in his old School as well as curate to
Wilson, and overworked, to the injury of his health. He was
troubled with a 'grievous cough' in 1623, for which he was
attended by Doctor Hall, and of which he died in April 1624,
aged twenty-four. Hall records in his case-book, *Multa frustra
tentata, placide cum Domino dormiit. Fuit boni indolis et
linguarum expertus, et pro juveni omnifariam doctus.*[3]

The Chancel was pronounced 'ruinous' in 1618, the Corporation resolved 'to bestow some charges' on keeping it
'dry' in 1619, and they were presented by Quyney and the
churchwardens (one of whom was Richard Tyler) for its
'decay' in April 1621. In 1621–2 the walls were 'mended' and
'painted' and the windows 'glazed', and the building was
presentable, for the first time since the Poet's interment, when

M.A., was appointed vicar of Stratford. Harris preached before
Parliament on 25 May 1642 on the eve of the Civil War.
[1] p. 36.   [2] *Register*, II. ii. 382, iii. 384.
[3] 'Many things were tried in vain; peacefully he slept with the Lord.
He was of a good wit, and was both grounded in the tongues and for a
young man in every way learned.'

his old friends and fellow-actors of the King's Company paid
their one and only visit to Stratford, presumably to see his
monument, in the Summer of 1622. Kemp, Pope, Phillips,
Bryan long since, and Burbage of late, were dead; but others
of his once matchless brotherhood survived—Lowin, Gough,
Tooley, Shanks, Underwood, and the editors of the forthcom-
ing Folio-edition of his Plays, Heminge and Condell. It is
significant of the change of mind in Stratford with regard to
the stage, as of the change in the character of the drama, that
even those men were forbidden to perform in the Gild Hall
and were paid 6s. as a *solatium*.[1]

22. THE POET'S BUST

THE King's Men may have had a hand in the Poet's monument. It was the work of Gerard Johnson (otherwise
Garret or Gheeraert Janssen), son of a Dutch tomb-maker of
the same name, resident in Southwark near the Globe. He
engraved John Combe's monument (in the north-east corner
of the Chancel at Stratford), and was probably recommended
for it by Shakespeare.[2] At Southwark the Poet's bust would
be at hand for his old friends to see and criticize. The inscription, in Latin and English, suggests London rather than
Stratford as its source:

> *Judicio Pylium, genio Socratem, arte Maronem,*
> *Terra tegit, populus maeret, Olympus habet.*[3]

> Stay Passenger, why goest thou by so fast?
> Read[4] if thou canst whom envious Death hath plac'd
> Within this monument: Shakespeare! with whom
> Quick Nature died, whose name doth deck this tomb

[1] 'To the King's Players, for not playing in the Hall, 6s.' Cham.
Acc. 10 Jan. 1623. See p. 75.
[2] Combe left 'three score pounds' for its erection.
[3] 'In judgement a Nestor, in intellect a Socrates, in art a Virgil: the
earth covers him, the people mourn him, Olympus has him.' For
Pylium see Ovid, *Amores*, iii. 7. 41, and Horace, *Carmina*, i. 15. 22.
[4] Decipher.

THE DROESHOUT PORTRAIT, 1609

THE BUST, 1616

Far more than cost; sith¹ all that he hath writ
Leaves living Art but page to serve his Wit.

Obiit anno domini 1616
Aetatis 53 die 23 Aprilis

The praise is enthusiastic. It tells of public grief, whatever
the new Court-taste and contempt for 'the many-headed
multitude', and of a mean, servile drama only fit to wait at the
table of the Master.

The Poet, bare-headed, looks up from his writing, his hands
resting on a cushion. The head was evidently taken from a
death-mask—the face is heavy, the eyes stare, the nose is
sharpened and the upper lip elongated by shrinkage of the
muscles and nostrils. The tall-domed forehead and crown are
bald, but the hair falls thickly over the ears. The eyes, under
high arched brows, are light hazel; the hair, moustache, and
short pointed beard are auburn.

The likeness to the Droeshout portrait is convincing. This
painting, which has triumphed over a generation of criticism,
and is the only genuine representation of Shakespeare beside
the bust, was the work also of an artist from the Low Countries,
Martin Droeshout of Brabant—in 1609, as we learn from the
name of the sitter and date (in the hand of a foreigner)² in the
left-hand corner at the top. The head, cut off by a starched
ruff from the tunic (which has evidently been entrusted to
an apprentice), resembles the bust in almost every particular
and is alive—the eyes are clear and penetrating, and the sensi-
tive mouth is ready to break into a smile. The more hair on the
crown and less on the lip and chin confirm the interval of six or
seven years.³

---

¹ The engraver has 'sieh', misreading *t* as *e*.
² Whence the somewhat perplexing script, which is neither Gothic
nor exactly cursive.   ³ See p. 79f.

23. 'OMNES RAPIT AEQUA DIES'

DOCTOR Hall was devoted to his puritan parish-church and vicar. He found time amid his duties as medical practitioner to serve as a churchwarden. He and his colleagues presented parishioners for 'loitering forth of Church at sermon time', 'sleeping in the belfry, with a hat on, upon the Sabbath', 'wearing a hat in church', 'being abroad, seen by the Constable, at sermon time', 'for late coming to church', and other offences. They report abuse by Goody Bromley, 'an ill-look woman' with the evil eye, of the wife of Adrian Holder. She threatened to 'overlook her and hern', and bade her 'Aroint thee, witch!' and 'get her home' (to Hell) 'or a would brush the motes forth of her dirty gown'. Shakespeare had listened to such spirited language.[1]

Hall cared less for the Corporation, and fell out with them in defence of Wilson, suffered in health perhaps by his unbridled championship. He died suddenly in November 1635. On his grave, next but one to Shakespeare's, were inscribed the lines, perhaps by the vicar:

> *Hallius hic situs est, medica celeberrimus arte,*
> *Expectans regni gaudia laeta Dei;*
> *Dignus erat meritis qui Nestora vinceret annis,*
> *In terris omnes sed rapit aequa dies.*[2]

On his widow's death these were added:

> *Ne tumulo quid desit, adest fidissima conjux,*
> *Et vitae comitem nunc quoque mortis habet.*[3]

Mistress Hall lived into the Civil War. Her son-in-law, Thomas Nash, was one of the few supporters of King Charles; and on this account, probably, New Place instead of the

---

[1] Misc. Doc. i. 160. Cf. *Macbeth*, I. iii. 6, and *Lear*, III. iv. 129.
[2] 'Hall is laid here, very renowned for medical skill, looking for the happy joys of the Kingdom of God. Worthy was he for his merits to outdo Nestor in years, but on earth a like Day lays hands on all.'
[3] 'Lest anything be wanting to his tomb, his most faithful wife is with him and the companion of his life he has now also in death.'

College (William Combe was both a puritan and a Parlia-
mentarian[1]) was selected for the entertainment of Queen
Henrietta in July 1643.[2] Nash, who had married Shakespeare's
granddaughter, Elizabeth Hall, on 22 April 1626, died suddenly on 4 April 1647, leaving no child, and appointing a
nephew his heir, Edward Nash—who became a captain in
Cromwell's army. Somewhat enigmatic verses were inscribed
on Thomas Nash's grave, next to Shakespeare's:

> *Fata manent omnes; hunc, non virtute carentem*
> *Ut neque divitiis, abstulit atra dies;*
> *Abstulit, at referet lux ultima. Siste, viator,*
> *Si peritura paras, per mala parta peris.*[3]

Is there anything personal, or mere pious punning, in the last
line?

His widow married in June 1649 John Barnard of Abington,
Northampton. Her mother died in July, and was buried beside
Doctor Hall. The epitaph is in English, and throws light on
Shakespeare's daughter:

> Witty above her sex, but that's not all:
> Wise to salvation was good Mistress Hall.
> Something of Shakespere was in that, but this
> Wholly of Him with whom she is now in bliss,
> Then, passenger, hast ne'er a tear
> To weep with her that wept with all
> That wept, yet set herself to cheer
> Them up with comforts cordial?
> Her love shall live, her mercy spread.
> When thou hast ne'er a tear to shed.

[1] *Symonds Diary*, Camden Soc., p. 191 f. He compounded for his
refusal of a coronation knighthood in 1626, and was presented with
his brother for recusancy in 1640.
[2] Chamberlain's Account 12 Jan. 1644.
[3] 'The Fates await all. This man, not wanting in virtue, as neither in
riches, the Black Day carried off—carried off, but the Light at Last
shall bring again. Stay, passenger; if thou preparest perishable things,
by evil fruits thou perishest.'

The writer, who may have been Alexander Beane, the able minister appointed to the Church by Cromwell,[1] does not attribute saving grace to a player and writer of plays; but his testimony to the 'wit', or quick intelligence, of Susanna Shakespeare, and to her pious benevolence, is emphatic and valuable evidence. 'Weep with them that weep' is from Romans xii. 15; 'wise to salvation' is from 2 Timothy iii. 15: 'Thou hast known the holy Scriptures of a child, which are able to make thee wise unto salvation through the faith which is in Christ Jesus.' We conclude that Shakespeare and Anne Hathaway brought up their children religiously.

Judith would need her faith. She had trouble with her husband at the *Cage*, the victim no doubt of his calling. She lost her children, her eldest boy, Shakespeare Quyney, in infancy, her other sons in early manhood, Richard and Thomas Quyney, within a month of each other in 1639. She lived into the Restoration, dying in 1662, aged 77, shortly before the induction of the conforming vicar, John Ward, who had recorded in his diary the intention to visit her.[2] Had he met her he would have handed down something better than his few and feeble memoranda of her father.[3] Apparently she was not interred within the Chancel. At the Restoration John Barnard was created a baronet, and for the last eight or nine years of her life Shakespeare's granddaughter was Lady Barnard. She

---

[1] Cromwell halted at Stratford, on his way to his 'Crowning Mercy' at Worcester, and wrote here a characteristic letter (dated 27 Aug. 1651, just a week before his rout of Charles and his Scotsmen) to the 'dubitating' Lord Wharton: 'The Lord's work needs *you* not, save as He needed the ass's beast to show His humility, but you need *it*, to declare your submission and own yourself the Lord's and His people's.' Thirty thousand men were with him and upwards of eighty thousand were ready to join him if need be, so overwhelming was popular feeling on the side of the Parliament (Carlyle, *Cromwell's Letters and Speeches*, pp. 288–90).

[2] *Diary*, Severn, p. 184 ('to see Mistress Queeny').

[3] *Ib.* 183 f. He adds, wisely, 'Remember to peruse Shakespeare's plays.'

died at Abington in 1670. Her husband was a scholar. John Howes, the minister of Abington, Fellow of Gonville and Caius College, Cambridge, called him his Maecenas, *splendidissimo patrono suo semper colendo bonarum literarum.*[1] He died in 1674. The inventory of his goods includes:

'In the Study: desks, chests, cabinets, trunks, and boxes, £5. 1. 6; all the plate there, £29. 10. 0; in rings, jewels and a watch £30; all the books, £29. 11. 0. In the Parlour: all the pictures there, £5. 10. 0. In the Best Chamber: pictures and andirons £2. In the Little Chamber: pictures, hangings, table and a carpet £6. A rent at Stratford-upon-Avon £4. Old goods and lumber at Stratford-upon-Avon, £4.'[2]

What became of these books and pictures? Little seems to have been left at New Place in 1674. Sir Edward Walker purchased the house next year.

24. THE DROESHOUT PORTRAIT AND ENGRAVING

THE portrait may be seen, and should be studied, at the Memorial Library in Stratford. On the elm panel has been laid a white gesso ground (whitening, or slaked plaster, and size), several coats. Over this when dry has been scumbled a thin warm red glaze, probably Indian red and a little umber in oil, after the practice of Flemish painters of the period. It is possible that this warm ground, which has been scumbled rather unevenly, suggested to some critics a portrait beneath. It shows through more in certain places than in others. Upon it has been painted the portrait in oil or oil varnish. In drying under the influence of time it has become very horny and cracked, separating at the slightest provocation from the gesso ground. The head has been prepared in a thick underpainting, probably in monochrome, and finished with glazes and thin paint.

[1] *Christ God-Man*, 1657.   [2] New Shak. Soc. Trans. 1880–5, pt. ii.

This portrait is obviously the original of the engraving in the Folio of 1623—the effort of 'Martin Droeshout junior', a young man of two and twenty years of age, and unequal to his task. His relationship to the painter (he was his nephew) is almost his sole qualification. The nose is too broad at the top and snubbed at the end, the forehead is bulbous as if the Poet died of water on the brain. The left eye is larger and lower than the right. Of the ear, because little or nothing was visible in the portrait, the young engraver, having to fall back on knowledge, makes a sorry mess. Subsequent efforts to improve the likeness of the engraving to the portrait, as appears from different stages of the plate, by the addition of shadows on the ruff and deepening of them on the brow, emphasize the want of resemblance and the unskilful hand.

Ben Jonson flattered, or forgot the engraving in elaborating his own verse, when he dared to say of the artist:

> O could he but have drawn his wit
> As well in brass as he hath hit
> His face, the print would then surpass
> All that was ever writ in brass!

This is ingenious but untrue—like his epigram on Shakespeare's learning, 'little Latin, less Greek'. The engraving is one of the many defects of the Folio.

DROESHOUT ENGRAVING OF SHAKESPEARE, 1623

A unique early state of the plate

DROESHOUT ENGRAVING OF SHAKESPEARE, 1623

From the original Bodleian First Folio

INDEX

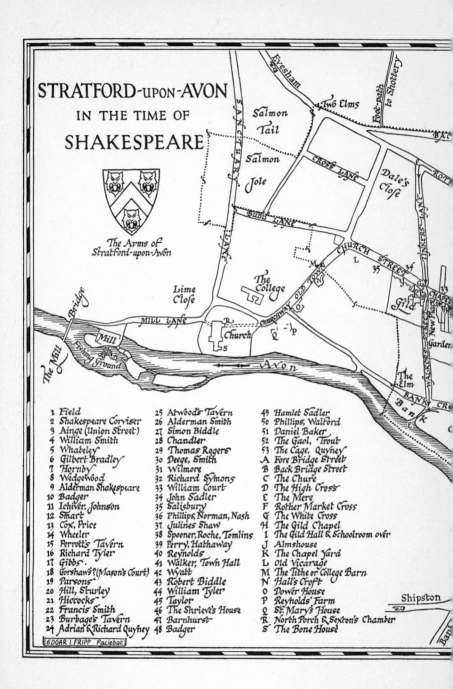

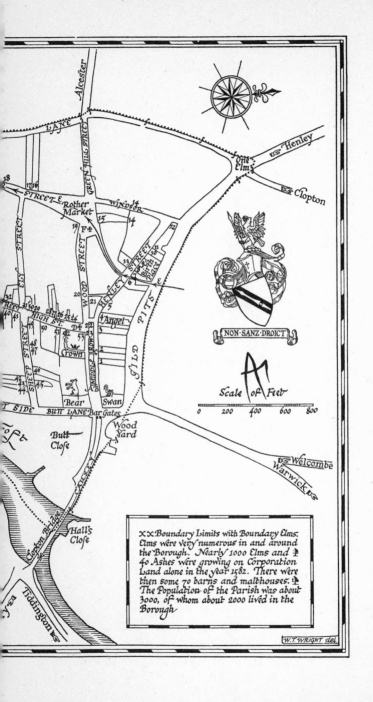

Alcester

LANE

GREEN HILL STREET

Henley

One Elms

Clopton

18 17 16

STREET E

Rother Market

WINDSOR

14

19 F 15 14

STREET G

WOOD STREET

13

HENLEY STREET

BIRTH PLACE

12

6 E

20 21

32 31 30 29 28 27 26 25 24

HIGH ST. D

CHAPEL ROW

Angel

23 22

Crown

22

2

42 43 44

48 47

46

45

Bear

B

A

Swan

GILD PITS

WEST SIDE

BUT LANE   Bar Gates

Butt Close

Wood Yard

Welcombe

Warwick

Clopton Bridge

Hall's Close

Tiddington

NON · SANZ · DROICT

A

Scale of Feet

0   200   400   600   800

XX Boundary Limits with Boundary Elms.
Elms were very numerous in and around
the Borough. Nearly 1000 Elms and
40 Ashes were growing on Corporation
Land alone in the year 1582. There were
then some 70 barns and malthouses.
The Population of the Parish was about
3000, of whom about 2000 lived in the
Borough

W.T. WRIGHT del.

Af